GADSDEN

CITY OF CHAMPIONS

This early photograph shows Broad Street looking west from Third Street. The giant clocktower of the Etowah County Courthouse is visible on the right and the Commercial Hotel is on the left.

THE
MAKING OF AMERICA
SERIES

GADSDEN

CITY OF CHAMPIONS

MIKE GOODSON

ARCADIA
PUBLISHING

ISBN 978-0-7385-2375-0

Published by Arcadia Publishing,
Charleston SC, Chicago IL, Portsmouth NH, San Francisco CA

Printed in the United States

Library of Congress control number: 2001099610

For all general information contact Arcadia Publishing at:
Telephone 843-853-2070
Fax 843-853-0044
E-Mail sales@arcadiapublishing.com
For customer service and orders:
Toll-Free 1-888-313-2665

Visit us on the Internet at www.arcadiapublishing.com

CONTENTS

ACKNOWLEDGMENTS

I am indebted to several people who have done much over the past years to record the city of Gadsden's rich and colorful history. Several individuals have preserved different events in this city's history in a variety of ways—from photographs to written words—that have helped to make this publication possible. Several important organizations have also been diligently at work for many years preserving and recording our local history, including the Etowah Historical Society and the Alabama City Historical Association. Specifically, I would like to acknowledge Linda Parker, who has restored the John Riley cabin, which was originally located at Double Springs.

Some important individuals have recorded Gadsden's history in written words including Charlie Boman, Will Martin, Bob "Ginger" Johnson, and Joe Barnes. Adolph Lebourg had a unique gift with a camera and recorded everyday life in downtown Gadsden. This gift has given many people a glimpse of life in the City of Champions during the 1920s through the 1950s.

Probably the single-most important attempt to record the history of Gadsden is in the form of a collection of photographs that have been amassed by local historian Bob Scarboro. Over the years, Scarboro has built an unbelievable collection of over 6,000 vintage photographs of Gadsden and surrounding Etowah County that date back into the mid- to late 1800s. Photographs from this collection have been used to illustrate many books on the North Alabama area, including two books in the *Images of America* series. The books on Etowah County were co-authored by Scarboro and myself. Most of the illustrations contained in the pages of this work came from this priceless collection, and I owe a great debt of gratitude to the owner of it.

A special note of thanks is also extended to Barbara Reed and the staff of the Gadsden Public Library, without whose help this book would not have been possible. The immense resources of the Gadsden Public Library, including Gadsden newspapers dating back to 1867, have made researching this city's history an exciting journey.

There are many other people who have helped to make this possible. For anyone who has taken time to share a story on the early days of Gadsden or a cherished photograph that has been handed down for many generations, I am grateful.

And finally, a special note of thanks to Ann, who has spent untold hours typing, proofreading, and correcting these pages.

INTRODUCTION

The City of Gadsden, Alabama, known as the "City of Champions," began as a dream. The dream began with three men who had moved to the small stagecoach stop on the banks of the Coosa River known as Double Springs.

Double Springs was a small settlement that consisted of several log dwellings, a store, a school, a post office, and a small stagecoach stop where weary travelers could rest while traveling between Jacksonville and Huntsville. John Riley built the first dwelling at Double Springs before selling to Gabriel Hughes in 1840. The coming of Gabriel and Asenath Hughes, followed by his brother Thomas Hughes, eventually brought about the founding of a new town. John S. Moragne joined forces with the Hughes brothers to survey a new town that would eventually grow into the city known today as Gadsden.

The new town began to grow when the first steamboat made its voyage slowly down the Coosa River. The USM *Coosa*, piloted by Captain James Lafferty, passed through the area and stopped near the site of the new town. An attempt was made to name the new city Lafferty's Landing, although the honor was declined. The name Gadsden was chosen in honor of James Gadsden, a former soldier and statesman who had passed through the area with Andrew Jackson several years earlier. Gadsden was at that time associated with the railroad and it was thought that this would bring a major railroad through the area.

The town of Gadsden grew at a slow pace until the ravages of the Civil War struck the area. It was at this time that a young girl, Emma Sansom, wrote her name in the history books in an incident that would take place at Black Creek. It was also at this time that John W. Wisdom emerged as the "Paul Revere of the South."

Following this war, the small village of Gadsden began to grow at an accelerated rate. Several astute businessmen, including Colonel Robert B. Kyle, brought major businesses to Gadsden. Kyle had a hand in most of the large companies operating in Gadsden during the late 1800s and early 1900s. Another great business mind to come to Gadsden was that of Captain James M. Elliott Jr. Captain Elliott created hundreds of jobs in Gadsden with the founding of the Elliott Car Works and the Elliott Peach Orchard. Captain Elliott and Colonel Kyle also founded Alabama City, which would later become a part of Gadsden.

The City of Gadsden continued to grow although destructive fires hit the small town on several occasions. Many businesses were destroyed, while others emerged from the ashes of these fires.

Several individuals also came to Gadsden who would contribute much to the growth of this small city. One such individual was Judge John H. Disque, who spent most of his life trying to build a free public school system in Gadsden.

The early days of the twentieth century saw a large amount of riverboat traffic between Gadsden and Rome, Georgia, with at least 40 boats making this trip weekly. Many of these colorful riverboat captains called Gadsden "home." Riverboat traffic slowly came to a close by the early 1920s when improved highways made riverboat travel unprofitable.

Gadsden sent her sons into battle during the days of World War I when a large number of Etowah County residents became part of the famous "Rainbow Division" serving in Europe. These brave young men who were originally part of the Alabama National Guard would be remembered when the first automobile traffic bridge was built over the Coosa River at Gadsden. This bridge was named the Memorial Bridge in honor of those who had served in the military.

Gadsden also tolerated a time of economic hardship during the Great Depression, following Black Friday and the stock market crash of 1929. Life slowly began to return to normal when the outbreak of World War II plunged Gadsden and Etowah County into a wartime economy.

In the days before and during World War II, new industry came to Gadsden that brought hundreds of jobs to the Gadsden Ordnance Plant and civilian jobs to Camp Sibert. Following the war, the area saw a return to normalcy and a time of extraordinary growth when Gadsden's fighting men returned home.

The days following the war were a time of great development for the city of Gadsden. Businesses returned to normal with record employment seen at the mills in Gadsden as well as at the steel plant and Goodyear. Movie theaters sprang up throughout the city, and the first drive-in theater opened. Happy days appeared to have arrived in Gadsden, and its growth accelerated into the 1950s.

It was during this time, however, that Gadsden lost two of its larger employers when the Coosa Thatcher Company's Sauquiot Spinning Mill and the Dwight Manufacturing Company closed. These closings sent a jolt through the Gadsden economy that affected hundreds of workers.

Gadsden became known as the "City of Champions" during the late 1950s due to the success of the Emma Sansom band and several local sports teams. This name was suggested by local radio personality Charlie Boman and would apply to the city throughout the remaining days of the twentieth century.

Gadsden also saw a time of uncertainty with the rumors of plant closings at Goodyear and the eventual shutting down of Gadsden's giant steel plant. The closing of Gulf States Steel meant that hundreds of Gadsden residents faced the difficulties of unemployment.

Gadsden also witnessed changes over the years in the form of municipal government. These changes saw the young city move from an intendant and alderman style of leadership to a mayor-council form of city government. Later, the City chose a commission form of government, and then returned to a mayor-council form of government to make the full circle.

Voted one of the most livable cities, Gadsden has been blessed with exceptional leadership over the years. This leadership has propelled Gadsden from a small village on the banks of the Coosa River to the "City of Champions" and an All-America City.

1. Indian Lore and Legend

For many years the only inhabitants to live in the area today known as Gadsden were members of the Creek and Cherokee Indian Nations. During the late 1700s and early 1800s, this area was part of the Mississippi Territory. Part of the land of Etowah County was considered neutral ground among the different Indian tribes that lived in this area. These Indian villages grew along the beautiful Coosa River, which brought life to the area and would eventually bring the first white settlers.

Of the many Indian villages located along the banks of the Coosa River, probably the most famous was the land of Chief Little Turkey, or "Turkey's Town." This Cherokee stronghold later became known as Turkeytown and stretched from near Centre in Cherokee County to just south of the present site of Gadsden in Etowah County, where the Coosa River and Wills Creek meet.

General Andrew Jackson passed through this area in a southerly direction during the War of 1812, cutting what is known as the Strother Road to Fort Strother at Ten Islands on the Coosa River and, from that point, marching to the battles of Tallassahatchee, Horse Shoe Bend, and Talladega. On his return from these battlefields, he marched to Turkeytown, crossing Wills Creek at what is known as Jackson's Ford, 2.5 miles from Gadsden, and passing through where Gadsden now stands. At Turkeytown, he concluded a treaty with the Cherokee Indians. In December 1832, the Creek and Cherokee Indians met on a large field near the banks of the Coosa River to settle a dispute over their lands near Gadsden. Rather than fighting to settle this problem, the Indians played a form of stick ball similar to modern-day lacrosse. The stake to the winners was a strip of neutral territory 4 miles wide on the boundary line between the Creek and Cherokee Nations, and this land was to be taken from the losing side. The contest was decided in favor of the Creeks. Future disputes between these two nations were settled on this field known as Ball Play near the present-day city of Gadsden. Some of the white settlers in the area were on hand to watch some of these contests.

In 1836, part of the Creeks, under the leadership of Neomicka, Neomathla, and Jim Henry commenced hostilities against white settlers in the area but surrendered in June of the same year. The leading men of the hostile party were taken prisoner and sent west in chains. Opathleola and Jim Boy, friendly Creek chiefs with 1,400 Creek warriors, were fighting alongside the whites during this campaign. All the hostile party was removed in

1836, and the friendly portion of the Creeks was removed in 1837. The Cherokees were removed in 1838. They were all collected at Ross Landing, now Chattanooga, by the government of the United States, then carried west to the Indian Territory. The Cherokee Chief Stan Wattie, who later served as a Confederate States general in the Trans-Mississippi Department during the Civil War, was born at Turkeytown in this county.

Today, many artifacts are found along the banks of the Coosa River from Centre to Whorton Bend near Gadsden. Arrowheads, pieces of pottery, and small beads can still be uncovered while walking along the riverbanks or searching through freshly plowed fields in and around the area known as Ball Play. These small artifacts are a reminder of two proud Indian nations that were the earliest residents of the future city of Gadsden.

Probably the best-known story about the days of the Indians living in the Gadsden area dates back to just after the Revolutionary War. It was during this time that the legend of Noccalula was born. This legend was first printed in the pages of the *Gadsden Times* in 1869 and has grown over the years. The story has been enjoyed as a legend for more than 100 years—but is this simply a legend or a story of fact?

Black Creek Falls is a beautiful waterfall in the foothills of Lookout Mountain overlooking the city of Gadsden below. This scenic area has been one of Gadsden and Etowah County's most valuable natural resources since the city's early beginning. The name of Black Creek Falls was later changed to Noccalula Falls in memory of Princess Noccalula.

Indian arrowheads, such as these, are occasionally found along the banks of the Coosa River in and around Gadsden.

Black Creek Falls, or Noccalula Falls, is located on Lookout Mountain in Gadsden.

Princess Noccalula, or Nohalula as the legend goes, was probably the daughter of Chief Little Turkey of the Cherokee Indians. The legend states that long ago on a mountain summit within sight and sound of a rushing waterfall lived a great Indian chief whose young daughter Noccalula was known far and wide for her beauty and loveliness of character. Many braves of the Cherokee Nation sought the hand of Noccalula in marriage from the old chief. The only one favored by the father of Noccalula was the rich chief of a powerful neighboring tribe. This wealthy chief had much to offer for the hand of the beautiful princess. Noccalula pleaded her case before her father that her heart had already been given to a young brave from her own tribe. This young brave was a fearless and valiant warrior but had little wealth to offer for the hand of the lovely princess. Noccalula's pleas fell on deaf ears and her lover was driven from the tribe. A marriage agreement was reached and plans were made for Princess Noccalula to wed the chief of the neighboring tribe.

The day for the wedding soon arrived and a great feast was prepared. The beautiful Princess Noccalula was adorned in colorful wedding robes and all preparations were made for the wedding. The Indian maiden was faced with a decision of monumental proportions. The dilemma of seeing her young brave driven from the tribe and facing marriage to an Indian chief that she did not love was too great for the young Noccalula. The reality that her father had entered into a marriage contract for wampum and horses would drive Noccalula to take the only way out that she could find. Overcome with grief, she quietly slipped away from the wedding feast and went to the place that she had enjoyed on many occasions. She went to the picturesque waterfall to sit and ponder her future and what course of action she could take. Heartbroken at the turn her life had taken, she reached her final tragic decision. Quietly, she stood up and walked to the edge of the deep gorge next to the waterfall.

In a brief instance, it was all over. The beautiful Princess Noccalula had taken her last step into eternity and legend. By the time her absence had been discovered at the wedding feast, it was too late to stop Noccalula. Her body was discovered a short time later floating in the creek below the falls. The old Indian chief was heartbroken to learn the fate of his lovely daughter. The chief gave the name "Noccalula Falls" to this great gorge, a name still used today.

The legend of Noccalula was generally regarded as a colorful story for many years. The basic storyline closely coincided with several other Cherokee legends that were told throughout the Southeast, from North Carolina to Alabama. This story slowly moved from legend to history with the discovery of Indian writings on the rocks located below the falls. These writings told a story that closely resembled the tale of Noccalula. These writings, when translated, related the tragic death of a beautiful Cherokee maiden known as Alivilda. She reportedly jumped to her death in 1827.

Is the tragic story of Princess Noccalula a modern legend or an actual event from the early history of the land that would eventually become the city of Gadsden? Many discoveries of Indian artifacts in this area lead to the belief that this legend actually took place.

By the year 1838, the removal of the Indians to the west had begun in earnest. White settlers who had been infiltrating the Etowah County area for years arrived in greater numbers once the removal of the Indians began. The land known as Turkey Town and Ball Play was soon settled by white settlers moving into the area from North Carolina, South Carolina, and Georgia. Portions of the former lands of Chief Little Turkey of the Cherokee Nation are today part of the City of Gadsden. The Indian heritage that made up the early beginnings of Gadsden is steeped in legend, but more and more evidence is being uncovered to point to these early legends as fact.

Although most of the Indian inhabitants of Gadsden had been removed, a few remained and intermarried with white settlers. A descendant of one of these marriages played a prominent role in the founding of the town—his name was John Riley. About 1825, Riley built a log cabin near a spring that became part of Gadsden, and this cabin served as his home for the next several years. Riley later sold it to William Walker. The first house built in this area, Riley's cabin has survived for more than 175 years.

The Riley cabin became an important stagecoach stop on the Huntsville-to-Rome stage route and was known as Double Springs because of its location near two natural springs. The cabin eventually housed the first post office in the area, which was established in 1836, and also the first school. William Walker performed the duties as the

This is the original cabin of John Riley, which was moved and restored to its original appearance. The cabin was a stagecoach stop at Double Springs. (Courtesy of Linda Parker.)

first postmaster of the small village, which served as an important relay station on the stage line from Rome to Huntsville. Walker sold this cabin to a couple named Gabriel and Asenath Hughes, who also played a major part in the founding of the new town located near Double Springs. At the time that the Gabriel Hughes family, along with Joseph Hughes, moved to Double Springs, there were probably only three families living at this little settlement.

John D. McMichael came to the small village of Double Springs as the settlement's first schoolteacher. A man of mystery and intrigue, little was known about his past, though he was believed to be of a Southern aristocratic background. When the first post office was established at the new town of Gadsden, McMichael became that city's first postmaster.

Gabriel Hughes was born in Haywood County, North Carolina, on February 8, 1802, and he mined gold in Georgia before marrying Asenath D. Young in 1832. Asenath and Gabriel Hughes, along with his brother, moved to Jacksonville, Alabama, in 1838 and on to the small settlement of Double Springs in 1840. At this time the small settlement had only a general store, grocery store, and post office. In 1842, Gabriel and Joseph Hughes began buying all the land from the foot of Lookout Mountain to the Coosa River and

(LEFT) *Gabriel Hughes would come to Double Springs in 1840. He, along with his brother Joseph, and John S. Moragne would draw up the original survey for the City of Gadsden.* (RIGHT) *John S. Moragne owned 80 acres of land that extended across the present business district of downtown Gadsden.*

down the river to the mouth of Wills Creek. Adjacent to the Hughes' property were 80 acres of land owned by John S. Moragne that extended across the present business section of Gadsden on the west bank of the Coosa River.

Gabriel Hughes, Joseph Hughes, and John S. Moragne had a long-range dream for this property. In the next few months, plans slowly unfolded to bring a new town into existence. This town began near the banks of the beautiful Coosa River and was slowly extended in every direction. These events also saw the pioneer settlement of Double Springs slowly begin to fade away. The small village of Double Springs had served an important part in the early history of the town—this relay station for stagecoaches had brought the founders of Gadsden to the area.

2. From Double Springs to Gadsden

The small stage stop at Double Springs was an important relay station on the long stagecoach ride from Huntsville to Rome in 1840. This was a welcome stopping point where passengers could eat a warm meal and take a break from the long, dusty trail.

Gabriel Hughes had purchased this property in 1840 and became the postmaster at Double Springs. Hughes had plans for this small settlement that would have far-reaching effects for many years to come.

At the time of Gabriel Hughes's arrival in Double Springs, the only traffic on the Coosa River was in the form of Indian canoes and large flatboats. These flatboats were used to transport goods and travelers up and down the river from settlement to settlement between Georgia and Alabama. Travel on the river, however, was slow and the stagecoach was considered the quickest and most efficient way to travel. This all changed quickly on the morning of July 4, 1845, when an event unfolded that signified great changes for Double Springs.

For many months, three enterprising individuals had been dreaming of and planning for a new city located near the settlement of Double Springs. Gabriel Hughes, John S. Moragne, and Joseph Hughes had been surveying a new city located on the banks of the Coosa River. This city would be located on 120 acres of land at the present site of downtown Gadsden bounded from First Street on the east to Seventh Street on the west and from Locust Street on the north to Chestnut Street on the south. The plans for this city would then extend in each direction on land that had been purchased by the Hughes brothers and Moragne. This was quite a long-range vision for development, and it received a great boost on the morning of July 4, 1845.

The early morning quietness of this Independence Day was broken by a great noise, the likes of which had never been heard on this part of the Coosa River. Several long, loud blasts of a steam whistle caused the settlers of Double Springs to come running to the riverbank to see what was making such a great commotion. The sight that greeted the startled spectators was one that had never been seen on this river. The horrified onlookers saw an unusual looking ship making its way toward Double Springs and to the area that had been surveyed for another city. As the boat came closer, belching steam and puffs of white smoke, the curious onlookers caught their first glimpse of the first of many steamboats that would pass through this area from Rome to Greensport. The *Coosa* was making its maiden voyage, clearing the river of snags and opening the Coosa River to steamboat traffic.

This voyage of the *Coosa* was carefully planned by the steamboat's captain, Captain James Lafferty, and the surveyors of this new town near Double Springs. The boat had on its wheelhouse the name "USM *Coosa*," which also indicated that it carried the United States mail. For many years, the *Coosa* made this trip delivering mail to the area. The steamboat had been built on the banks of the Ohio River at Cincinnati by Captain Lafferty and had taken a roundabout journey before reaching the Coosa River. It was brought down the Mississippi River to New Orleans and, from there, had steamed to Mobile, where it came up the Alabama and Coosa Rivers to Wetumpka. There, it was dismantled and transported overland to Greensport, 30 miles south of Gadsden, and put together again before Captain Lafferty sailed it up the river to the present-day site of Gadsden.

The *Coosa* slowly came to a stop at the west bank of the river near the present site of the Memorial Bridge. Captain Lafferty and his crew were greeted by Gabriel Hughes, Joseph Hughes, and John S. Moragne. Along with Joseph Rhea, these men owned the majority of the acreage in the original survey of this new city. The surveyors of the city offered to name the new town "Lafferty's Landing" in honor of James Lafferty. Captain Lafferty declined this honor and a new name for the town was sought.

Colonel James Gadsden was a famous soldier and statesman from South Carolina. The City of Gadsden was named in his honor.

Joseph Rufus Hughes, the son of Gabriel and Asenath Hughes, was born on March 14, 1842.

The name chosen for the town was "Gadsden" in honor of Colonel James Gadsden, a greatly admired South Carolinian who was a personal friend of the Hughes family and Moragne. Colonel Gadsden had passed through the area with Andrew Jackson. Serving later as United States minister to Mexico, he negotiated the famous Gadsden Purchase in 1853, which added portions of present-day Arizona and New Mexico. It was believed that Colonel Gadsden, who was pushing for a trans-continental railroad, would bring a major railroad through the city. This, however, never happened.

Several choice lots were offered to Captain Lafferty if he would make a permanent landing at Gadsden. The new town slowly began to grow as people moved to the area. On June 17, 1846, lots in Gadsden were offered for sale in the Cherokee *Sentinel*, an early newspaper.

During the early days of the planning and founding of Gadsden, the first white child was born in the small village of Double Springs. Joseph Rufus, the son of Gabriel and Asenath Hughes, was born on March 14, 1842. Hughes later became one of the area's more prominent citizens, serving in a variety of businesses over the years.

Gabriel Hughes worked for many years to build the town that he had envisioned several years before. In 1857, Hughes moved near Attalla to a two-story Colonial home, where he resided until his death in 1886.

Another prominent name in the early days of Gadsden was that of General Daniel Clower Turrentine. Born in Milledgeville, Georgia, on October 18, 1807, Turrentine

The Turrentine Inn was the first hotel in the Gadsden area. This hotel (and tavern) was built near the riverboat landing.

General Turrentine built a huge home 1.5 miles west of the Turrentine Inn. Portions of this farm became Turrentine Avenue.

married Caroline Elizabeth Lucy on December 3, 1837, and moved to Dekalb County in 1839. He moved his family to the Double Springs area in 1843 and built an inn and store near the landing chosen by Captain James Lafferty for the *Coosa* in 1845. The inn and tavern eventually served six stage lines that ran past it.

General Turrentine was also concerned with the spiritual welfare of the small community. He started the first Sunday school in the area, and this became the nucleus of all religious denominations in the hamlet. In 1845, he and his wife were the guiding force in the organization of the First Methodist Church. The members of this church worshiped in a schoolhouse on the south side of Broad Street between Fourth and Fifth Streets. Later, a building was erected between Locust and Broad Streets that was used as a Union Church, serving all denominations. The first church built on the present site of the First Methodist Church was begun in 1854 under the supervision of General Turrentine. The land for this church was donated by Gabriel Hughes.

In 1851, the Turrentine family purchased a large farm about 1.5 miles west of the steamboat landing and Turrentine Inn. On this land, General Turrentine built an imposing residence. Portions of the farm later became Turrentine Avenue. The many giant oak trees lining this street were planted by the general's son-in-law Major R.O. Randall. General Turrentine, known affectionately as "Uncle T," was a tireless worker in his church throughout his life. Mrs. Turrentine passed away on July 24, 1881, and the beloved General Turrentine passed away two years later. The Turrentines had a total of 14 children.

General Daniel Clower Turrentine started the first Sunday school in the area and was the guiding force in the founding of the First Methodist Church in 1845.

The beginnings of the Baptist church in Gadsden date back to August 23, 1855. It was on this day that a group of dedicated Baptist believers met with Reverend J.D. Renfro to organize the First Baptist Church of Gadsden. The organization of this church was assisted by Phillip Archer, who wrote the articles of faith. The church's first pastor was Reverend J.B. Appleton.

The congregation met in a small academy on Chestnut Street between Fourth and Fifth Streets. In 1858, the church purchased a lot on the northwest corner of Fifth and Broad Streets at a cost of $100, and the congregation erected its first church building in 1860. The six charter members of this church were A.W. Keeling, Memory H. Turner, Adeline Turner, Joseph Bevans, L. Best, and Melissa Cobb.

Another individual who played a prominent role in Gadsden's early growth was an astute businessman named Robert Benjamin Kyle. Colonel R.B. Kyle moved to the area when Gadsden was still a struggling town of only 150 citizens in 1857. Colonel Kyle brought years of experience in the mercantile, banking, and railroad fields that would prove valuable in attracting industry and business to the town.

Kyle was born in Leaksville, North Carolina, on May 24, 1826, and was educated in the common schools of North Carolina and Columbus, Georgia. In 1848, he married Mary Allen Thornton, daughter of Major Dozier Thornton of Columbus, Georgia. Colonel Kyle was active in the mercantile business in Columbus, Georgia, until 1850, at which time he sold his interest in the dry goods business and became involved with the wholesale grocery business until the spring of 1853.

In 1853, R.B. Kyle purchased a large plantation on the banks of the Coosa River in Cherokee County, Alabama. At this large plantation, Kyle engaged in planting in

Colonel R.B. Kyle purchased a large home from William and Susan Christopher and moved his family to this imposing dwelling.

connection with his father-in-law, Dozier Thornton. While living on the farm, Mary Thornton passed away in 1855. Colonel Kyle married Mary Virginia Nuckolls of Columbus, Georgia, in 1856, and in 1857, Kyle moved his family to Gadsden to engage in private banking and the mercantile business.

Colonel Kyle was active in many of the early businesses in the Gadsden area and also became very active in local politics and civic organizations. He was a successful businessman and amassed a small fortune by the early days of 1860. He purchased a large home from William and Susan Christopher that later became one of the most recognizable homes in Gadsden.

Gadsden was still only sparsely settled in the mid-1850s. Many of the little town's homes were built in the thickly wooded areas around the town's main business district. By the year 1851, one railroad passed through Gadsden to Tuscaloosa and on to Vicksburg, Mississippi. Gadsden had long been envisioned as a rail center, although the major railroads never came through the town. Gadsden did have daily stagecoach service to and from Jacksonville, Alabama. The steamboats from Rome, Georgia, to Greensport, Alabama, made their schedules compatible with the stagecoach and trains. These steamboats and the colorful captains who piloted them would be the lifeblood of the small town during its early days.

From the earliest days of steamboat trade on the Coosa River, the route from Rome, Georgia, to Gadsden and Greensport was one of the most important. Mail, freight, and passengers were transported between these towns on a regular basis. Rome was an important site for steamboat construction and was the headquarters for the Coosa River Steamboat Company. In 1849, this company purchased the USM *Coosa*. In 1855, one of

Riverboats that carried goods to and from Gadsden are tied at the wharf in Gadsden. The Sidney P. Smith, *the* Etowah Bill, *and the* Magnolia *are shown unloading cotton.*

Captain William M. Elliott, son of James M. Elliott Sr., stands next to the Hill City.

the most famous riverboat captains came to Rome to engage in steamboat construction. Captain Francis Marion Coulter of Freedom, Pennsylvania, was personally responsible for the construction of at least a dozen of the finest steamboats to ply the waters of the Coosa. The *Magnolia*, which made regular trips from Rome to Gadsden, was regarded as one of the largest and finest steamers constructed by Coulter.

Another famous name in steamboat construction was Captain James M. Elliott Sr. Elliott was born in 1825 and became a pioneer owner and operator of steamboats on the Coosa River. He was the owner of the *Alphretta*, *Laura Moore*, *Magnolia*, *Hill City*, and others. Elliott had two sons that also became famous riverboat captains. James M. Elliott Jr. and William M. Elliott were closely associated with travel on the Coosa River for many years. These riverboat captains and many others played an important role in the early development of the city.

Between the years of 1845 and 1860, the city of Gadsden grew from a small stagecoach stop to an important port on the Coosa River. The town was attracting new residents at a steady pace, and a variety of new businesses were also moving to the area. The 40 or more riverboats that traveled the Coosa brought a steady flow of goods and visitors to the new city. Gadsden was an evolving village when the events that unfolded during the next few years brought a change to the area. It began with the first rumblings of war in 1861.

3. Rumblings of War

Gadsden was a steady, growing village during the early days of 1860. National politics seemed hundreds of miles away to the 400 residents of Gadsden. However, on Christmas Eve, 1860, an election was held in Cherokee County to choose delegates to a convention in Montgomery that would have lasting effects on Gadsden and the rest of the South. At this time, the county that would one day become Etowah was divided among Cherokee, Blount, Dekalb, Calhoun, St. Clair, and Marshall Counties.

The delegates elected were Dr. John Perkins Ralls, John Potter, W.C. Whitlock, and H.C. Sanford—these men would make decisions that would write a turbulent chapter in the history of Gadsden and Alabama. On January 7, 1861, the convention called by Alabama Governor Andrew B. Moore met to decide whether or not Alabama should withdraw from the Union. Ralls voted with the majority and afterwards served two terms in the Confederate Congress in Richmond.

With the outbreak of the war, many Gadsden residents were quick to take up arms and join the Confederate forces. Colonel R.B. Kyle opened the first recruiting office in Gadsden for the Confederate Army and later saw action in Tennessee. After his health failed, he served the remainder of the war in the quartermaster corps in Columbus, Georgia. Other Gadsden residents fought gallantly during this four-year conflict. William P. Hollingsworth led Company D of the 19th Alabama Regiment valiantly into combat, and Isaac Moragne led a group of volunteers that joined the Confederate Army at Talladega.

Although the town was spared much of the horrors of this brutal conflict, on several occasions the war did touch the citizens of Gadsden. Two major events did unfold here and brought much attention to the small village of Gadsden. The first event to bring the war close to home took place near Gadsden on the morning of May 2, 1863.

Up until this date, little news of the war raging between North and South had reached the small village, but this would drastically change on this early spring morning, as two opposing armies were on a collision course to meet in or near Gadsden. Colonel Able Streight and 1,500 Union troops were heading east to capture and burn Rome, Georgia. Streight, however, was being pursued closely by Confederate Nathan Bedford Forrest and 500 Confederate cavalrymen. Streight had been ordered to burn and destroy everything of value in his path, although the approach of Forrest had changed most of Streight's plans.

Colonel R.B. Kyle, a very prominent citizen of Gadsden, served in the Confederate Army and also opened the first recruiting office for the Confederate Army in Gadsden. (Courtesy Alabama Department of Archives and History, Montgomery, Alabama.)

What unfolded on the morning of May 2 about 2 miles west of Gadsden played a major role in the Forrest-Streight saga, which would forever be remembered in the history of Gadsden. This event took place at the Sansom home near the banks of Black Creek.

Micajah and Levina Vance Sansom had moved to the Gadsden area from Social Circle, Georgia, in October 1852. With their large family of 12 children, the Sansoms settled near Black Creek and built a sizable farm. Micajah Sansom died on December 24, 1859, and was buried in a small private cemetery near the family home about 200 yards from Black Creek.

At the outbreak of the war, three of the Sansom children were still living at home with their widowed mother, including Rufus, age 22, who enlisted in the Confederate Army in 1861; Jennie, age 24; and Emma, age 15. Mrs. Sansom and her two daughters managed well on their large farm, and their success was due in part to the energy of Emma, who was a very attractive, young lady with a fair complexion, deep blue eyes, and auburn hair. Little did this young girl know the place history would have for her on the early morning of May 2, 1863.

The Sansoms were greeted by a beautiful sunrise that had replaced the stormy weather of the three previous days. Severe thunderstorms had brought several inches of rain to the area, and Black Creek, near the Sansom home, was almost out of its banks. Shortly after sunrise, the members of the Sansom family were startled to see hundreds of blue-clad calvary riding up to the family home. Rufus Sansom, who was home at the time, was taken prisoner and the Sansom home was searched for food and any guns or ammunition

Emma Sansom was a brave 15-year-old girl who gained fame when she showed Nathan Bedford Forrest a way to cross Black Creek as he was pursuing Colonel Abel Streight and his Union Cavalry.

that might be there. The only horse that was there was also taken by the Union soldiers. Colonel Streight and his men quickly mounted their horses and crossed the only bridge across the rain-swollen creek and rode off in the direction of Gadsden. Colonel Streight had the wooden bridge put to the torch to slow the pursuit of Forrest and his cavalry. Several of Streight's men were left behind on the east bank of Black Creek to attempt to slow Forrest down at the creek. When Forrest arrived a short time later, he found the bridge an inferno of flames.

As Forrest was approaching the bridge at Black Creek, Streight had reached the business district of downtown Gadsden. Streight leveled some buildings and burned the ferry across the Coosa River, which was owned by John W. Wisdom and R.B. Kyle. Streight would probably have burned the entire town except for the fact that the Confederates had closed the gap between the two armies. Streight quickly turned his attention back toward Rome, left the city, and moved on toward Cedar Bluff.

Forrest and his men were briefly detained at Black Creek trying to find another way to cross the swollen creek. Occasional gunfire from Yankee snipers on the opposite bank kept the Confederates searching for cover. General Forrest remembered the farmhouse that he and his men had passed near the creek. He and some of his men returned to the Sansom home to ask if there was another way to cross the creek. Upon his large white horse, Forrest was an imposing figure with his gray uniform and gray cape. He asked Mrs. Sansom, Jennie, and Emma about another bridge to cross the creek to continue his

This was the home of the Sansom family located near the banks of Black Creek just west of Gadsden in 1863.

pursuit of the Union raiders. Emma quickly stepped forward and told of a lost ford that the Sansom family used to move cattle across the creek. This was located upstream from the burning bridge.

Forrest asked if the girl would show him the location of this ford. Emma was willing do this, and Forrest lifted the brave 15-year-old girl onto the horse and galloped away toward the creek. Forrest, Sansom, and the large column of gray-clad troops began moving up the creek to the location of the crossing. A bullet from one of the Union snipers passed through Emma's skirt and Forrest quickly moved the brave girl behind him, saying that history would never find him hiding behind the skirt of a woman. Another sniper's bullet found its mark killing Robert Turner, one of Forrest's men. As the column of troops began to cross the creek, Colonel Streight's snipers were quickly rounded up and captured. Forrest returned Sansom to the safety of her home exclaiming that he had never seen such bravery throughout the entire war. The body of Robert Turner was also brought to the Sansom home and was buried in the family cemetery.

Forrest asked for a lock of Emma Sansom's hair and then quickly rode off to join his men in pursuit of Colonel Streight. The chase would move on through Turkeytown, where a brief skirmish was fought, and then on toward Cedar Bluff.

While these events were unfolding at Black Creek and Gadsden, another chapter was being written on Gadsden's role in the War between the States. John W. Wisdom was returning from making his rounds as a rural mail carrier when he found his ferryboat missing. This ferry was located at the present site of the Memorial Bridge near Broad Street. Wisdom found his ferry downstream drifting and burning, and when he learned what had happened, he set out over the next several hours to write his name in the history books.

John Wisdom returned to Gadsden about 3:00 p.m. on May 2 and was informed that Union troops were responsible for the destruction of his ferryboat. An irate Wisdom was determined that the Yankees were heading for Rome to capture that city. This important town was located 67 miles from Gadsden. Wisdom left Gadsden about 3:30 in the afternoon in his buggy and arrived in Rome some 11 hours later. He had made this trip using five horses and one mule, which he borrowed along the way. This ride was made over very rough terrain, as Wisdom was trying to avoid contact with the Union soldiers. As Wisdom rode through the streets of Rome in the early hours of the morning shouting that the "Yankees were coming," every citizen capable of bearing a firearm lined the streets to defend the city.

Wisdom's early morning warning of the approaching danger brought the town's residents out in numbers to defend their city. The bridge across the river leading into town was quickly lined with cotton bales to block the advance of Colonel Streight's men. These cotton bales were soaked in oil in case the bridge needed to be burned to stop the Union forces at the bridge. The city was prepared for battle when the 200 men of Streight's vanguard force arrived.

Two hours after Wisdom arrived in Rome, Union Captain Russell arrived to lay siege to the city. He found the river bridge, which was his main objective, lined with cotton bales, hay bales, and heavily armed citizens. The torches and the ear-piercing shouts from the city led Captain Russell to believe that a large Confederate army had already entered

John W. Wisdom gained fame as the "Paul Revere of the South" when he rode from Gadsden to Rome in 11 hours to warn of the approach of Colonel Abel Streight.

the city. Captain Russell quickly turned away without the first shot being fired. This was a devastating blow to Colonel Streight and his plans to capture Rome.

At 9:00 a.m. the following day, Colonel Streight stopped at the Lawrence place near Cedar Bluff. It was at this time that he learned of Captain Russell's failure to capture the bridge at Rome. Streight felt his only course of action was to cross the bridge and burn it, thereby halting Forrest's advance. Many of Streight's exhausted troops fell asleep, and Streight's plans were in disarray. It was at this time that Forrest overtook the Union army.

Forrest sent word to Streight that he wanted to talk of surrender. Streight and Forrest met at the Lawrence plantation, at which time Forrest asked for Streight's surrender. During the meeting, Forrest had columns of his cavalry circling the Lawrence place making it appear that he had hundreds of troops. Streight felt that his only recourse was to surrender to a superior force. As the Union soldiers surrendered their arms, it became obvious that Forrest had captured 1,466 Union soldiers with only about 500 men.

Forrest marched his prisoners on to Rome, where a grateful city treated the small Confederate force to a hero's welcome. John Wisdom was also honored by the city. He was given a reward of silver for his part in alerting the city of the impending danger and turning back Captain Russell's troops at the bridge.

Forrest returned to Gadsden on May 7 with several of his officers to spend the night at the home of Colonel and Mrs. R.B. Kyle. The following day, Forrest called on the home of Emma Sansom to formally thank her for her assistance in capturing Streight and saving Rome.

Emma Sansom was given a parcel of public land and an inscribed gold medal by the Alabama legislature. This presentation was made in a ceremony held at Turkeytown in December 1863. Sansom remained in the Gadsden area for several years. In 1864, she married Christopher Johnson, a former Confederate soldier. They moved to Texas in 1876 where Johnson served with the Texas Rangers and also farmed. Christopher Johnson passed away on May 27, 1887, followed by Emma on August 9, 1900. The bravery that this young 15-year-old girl exhibited on an early spring morning back in 1863 has been remembered throughout the ensuing years.

Another event during 1864 brought the war dangerously close to the people living in Gadsden, and this event could have turned the village into a major battlefield between the Blue and the Gray. It was on the morning of October 20, 1864, that an advance detachment of the 8th Alabama Cavalry of the Confederate Army crossed the Coosa River on the ferry near the present site of Broad Street and pitched camp on the block bounded by Broad, Second, Third, and Chestnut Streets. At that time, this block was a large wooded area. The residents of the town were amazed to see these members of the Confederate Army arriving for no apparent reason and without advance warning.

The following morning pontoon bridges were assembled across the river at Gadsden and Hokes Bluff, and a huge army began to cross the river and move into the Gadsden area. By night, an army of over 33,000 troops were camped in and around the small town.

This invading army was commanded by General John Bell Hood, who made his headquarters in the old First Baptist Church, which stood on the corner of Fifth and Broad Street, where the Center for Cultural Arts is now located. General Hood was joined by General Joseph Wheeler and his cavalry just before reaching Gadsden. General

The Lawrence house in neighboring Cherokee County was the site of Colonel Streight's surrender to Forrest. This landmark was destroyed in 1952.

P.G.T. Beauregard joined them at Gadsden to discuss Hood's plan to invade Tennessee. The three generals met for two days at the First Baptist Church to finalize the plans for this campaign.

While Hood, Wheeler, and Beauregard were in these planning sessions, the combined army, now totaling over 40,000 troops, were getting two days of much needed rest. The ragged army also received needed supplies and rations of food. The campfires in and around Gadsden could be seen for miles in many directions. After the distribution of the quartermaster's stores, the huge army was ready to once again march on toward the north and Nashville, Tennessee, to attempt to break the Union supply lines.

While the generals and their staff were meeting in Gadsden, Union General William T. Sherman and his more than 70,000 troops were marching toward Gadsden with every intention of fighting a main engagement. Sherman was as close as Cedar Bluff in nearby Cherokee County when he decided to end his pursuit of Hood and his Confederate troops. Sherman decided to turn his troops elsewhere and allow Hood to be dealt with in Tennessee.

On October 22, 1864, the army under the command of General Hood began its long march from Gadsden to Gunter's Landing. With bugles blasting and rebel yells filling the early morning air, the army left the small town. The plans were for Hood to meet General Nathan Bedford Forrest at Gunter's Landing, now Guntersville. Although Forrest never received his orders, these armies did come together and marched into disaster at Franklin, Tennessee.

For a brief two-day period, Gadsden had been home to a large invading army. General Joseph Wheeler and his men did stay behind to engage General Sherman, although Sherman turned away from Gadsden when he learned that Hood and his army had departed. Gadsden narrowly escaped being the scene of a major engagement between the Blue and Gray—an engagement that could have spelled disaster for the small town.

There was other significant Civil War activity in the Gadsden area. General James H. Clanton organized the 8th Alabama Calvary at Gadsden. This outfit was a greater terror to the residents of the area than the raiding Union soldiers. General Clanton used Gadsden's First Baptist Church as his headquarters during his stay in the area. When the church bell quit ringing on one occasion, an investigation was made into the church's belfry and a startling discovery was made. Several soldiers had stuffed the bell with cloth and set up a table and chairs to play poker for hours on end. When General Clanton left the Gadsden area, some of his men stole the silver communion service and the large church bell. Word was sent to General Clanton about the theft, and after a thorough search of his men, the silver service and bell were returned.

During the days of the war, other Confederate generals set up their headquarters in Gadsden. General John A. Whorton was headquartered in town for a brief period of time, and General Phillip D. Roddy carried out raids against Northern troops stationed along the Tennessee River from his headquarters in Gadsden.

Other Gadsden residents contributed to the war effort during the turbulent years between 1861 and 1865. The Keeling house, formerly the Turrentine Inn, was used as a hospital for wounded Confederate soldiers. When soldiers passed through town, they could stop here to receive medical attention from one of the doctors that was available.

The First Baptist Church was the scene of a meeting between Confederate Generals John Bell Hood, Joseph Wheeler, and P.G.T. Beauregard on October 20, 1864.

With the surrender of Confederate General Robert E. Lee at Appomattox Courthouse in April 1865, the nation breathed a sigh of relief that the long years of fighting were at an end. Many Gadsden residents came home to pick up the pieces of their lives and to put businesses and farms back in order. Several residents returned to a hero's welcome for their actions on the battlefield. Others, such as Emma Sansom and John W. Wisdom, had gained fame for their unique contributions to the war effort. Gadsden saw little actual combat during these years, although the war had come close to home on several occasions.

The city of Gadsden survived the most devastating war that the United States had ever seen and, at the end of the war, looked much like it had at the beginning. The small town still had a population of only about 400 citizens in the year 1865. In the next few years, however, Gadsden would go through a phase of growth and prosperity.

4. YEARS OF GROWTH: 1866 TO 1890

Following the Civil War, life returned to normal in the small town of Gadsden. The city had gone through this turbulent time pretty much untouched since very little of the war had actually come through the area. Many of Gadsden's sons returned to pick up the pieces of their lives. Colonel R.B. Kyle returned to seek the vast fortune he had lost during the previous four years. Although Gadsden still had only about 400 citizens, the small town would soon begin to grow at an accelerated rate.

The year 1867 saw the small village of Gadsden choose its first mayor, or "intendant" as the early mayors were called. The first intendant was Colonel R.B. Kyle, who was elected for a one-year term. The intendant, along with a board of aldermen, made the decisions and passed the ordinances that guided the small town through its first year of city government. Several intelligent men served as intendants during these first years.

During the early years, several colorful residents serve as mayor of Gadsden. Colonel R.B. Kyle served three one-year terms, in 1867, 1868, and again in 1872. L.W. Grant was elected mayor for 1869, and W.L. Cain was Gadsden's mayor in 1870, although he committed suicide while in office. W.B. Martin served as mayor in 1871, J.L. Cunningham in 1873, Dr. I.M. Stevens in 1874, Judge John H. Disque from 1875 to 1877, Joseph Bevans in 1878 and 1879, and W.H. Standifer from 1880 to 1881. In 1882, McDougald Nesbit was elected but died before taking office. Marcus Beeson took over as mayor but died while in office. J.T. Brooks was elected by the board of aldermen in July to complete the term.

By 1883, the Gadsden mayor was elected for a two-year term. J.T. Brooks was elected mayor in 1883, W.H. Standifer in 1885, John H. Disque in 1887, and John P. Ralls Jr. in 1889.

During the year of 1866, a new county was formed with Gadsden selected as the county seat. Baine County was formed from lands taken from Marshall, Dekalb, Cherokee, St. Clair, Calhoun, and Blount Counties. This county, formed by a special act of the state legislature, was short-lived, however, and was abolished one year later by the post-war military government imposed on the state of Alabama. Much resentment was felt about this new county and its name. William Baine was a popular Confederate leader from Cherokee County. Thomas Burgess served as the first sheriff of Baine County, and L.E. Hamlin as the first probate judge.

The county was re-established the following year with the same boundaries. The name chosen for the county this time was "Etowah" rather than Baine, with Gadsden once again as the county seat. Samuel Dillard was elected the first sheriff of Etowah County, and William Tallman, the first judge of probate. Court was held in the First Baptist Church on Broad Street until a courthouse was constructed on land located between Locust, Fourth, Court, and Broad Streets. This courthouse was built and paid for by Colonel R.B. Kyle and Captain W.P. Lay. On December 8, 1869, the contract to build Etowah County's first courthouse was awarded to Isaac P. Moragne. The structure was completed at a cost of $12,990.

The courthouse, erected in a grove of oak trees on property donated by Samuel Henry, had a large porch in front that was supported by four huge, fluted columns. The building was constructed of brick made by hand on the Gardner place, and the first floor of this courthouse was also paved with brick. By the year 1870, Gadsden was growing at a rapid rate. The town was now the county seat of Etowah County and had a new courthouse.

During the year 1868, John Harold Disque moved to Gadsden from New Orleans, where he was born on March 23, 1848. After moving to Gadsden, Disque studied law and was admitted to the bar in 1872. At various times during his career, he served as county solicitor, judge of Gadsden City Court, and later mayor. The contributions of this distinguished citizen were considerable but his contributions to the public schools of Gadsden during these early days were the greatest.

This is an artist's rendering of the first Etowah County Courthouse built between Broad, Court, Locust, and Fourth Streets. (Courtesy of Danny Crownover.)

Judge John H. Disque served as Gadsden's mayor from 1875 until 1877. He also served as the county solicitor and Gadsden City judge.

Following the Civil War, a number of private schools operated in Gadsden. Over the next several years, however, a need was felt for a free public school system, but it was not until February 1877 that the first public school opened. This school opened in the old academy building on Locust Street, and it offered five months of classes at no tuition cost to students. Approximately 60 students attended this first public school, conducted by A.D. Bailey. In 1880, the first public school structure was built on College Street.

Gadsden began to grow at a fast pace during the years following the war due greatly to the commerce on the Coosa River. The Coosa River is formed at Rome, Georgia, by a junction of the Etowah and Oostanaula Rivers, which flow to Gadsden and on to Wetumpka. An important stop on the route of commerce between Rome and Greensport, Gadsden became a busy port during the late 1800s, as steamboats were a major means of transportation for both passengers and goods.

An air of excitement usually filled the city when one of the riverboats arrived at the wharf on the west bank of the river. A variety of goods were transported between Gadsden and Rome, including thousands of bales of cotton, furniture, and the latest in fashions for the local merchants. Working at the riverboat landing was a heavy job for the many local "roustabouts" who spent their days loading and unloading boats.

By 1873, there were six steamers making regular trips from Rome to Gadsden and Greensport to transport the ever-increasing volume of goods. On March 13, 1873, the beautiful *Magnolia*, constructed by the Georgia and Alabama Steamboat Company, made her maiden voyage from Rome to Gadsden.

Probably the most famous riverboat captains on the Coosa River were brothers James M. Elliott Jr. and William M. Elliott. Captain James M. Elliott Jr. was born on November 12, 1854. He became involved with boats owned and operated by his father. Captain

William M. Elliott was born in 1862. Like his father and older brother, he engaged in steamboating following his graduation from college. He was the captain of several boats, including the *Sidney P. Smith*, *Magnolia*, *Hill City*, and others.

The *Magnolia* was the largest and most elaborate riverboat to make the voyage from Rome to Gadsden. Captain James Elliott Jr. was well known throughout the small city. People would scurry to the wharf to see the steamboat dock and unload its cargo of treasures. One Gadsden resident who usually made the trip to the riverboat landing was Nena Kyle, daughter of Colonel R.B. Kyle. When the whistle announced the arrival of the *Magnolia*, Nena would take her buggy to the landing to see Captain Elliott. Captain Elliott and Nena Kyle would later marry, and Elliott would become one of Gadsden's most successful businessmen.

The riverboat traffic on the Coosa River not only brought commerce and growth to the small village, but also a legend of a river monster that was sighted on several occasions. This serpent was seen by several prominent citizens of the surrounding area and was also reported by riverboat captains making the trip between Rome and Gadsden.

The first sighting of this strange creature was reported in the pages of the *Gadsden Times* on June 8, 1877. Marcus Foster, a respected citizen of Gadsden, was fishing in the vicinity of Ball Play Creek when he noticed a strange commotion near the opposite bank. As Foster crossed the river to get a closer look, he was amazed to find a serpent-like creature glaring at him. This startled the fisherman and he paddled his boat away from the creature. The large snake-like creature floated silently along the bank until it slipped under the water.

The City of Gadsden *is shown here leaving the wharf loaded with cotton. This was one of the many steamboats to make the trip from Rome to Gadsden.*

Marcus Foster later told of his experience rather reluctantly. Fearing public ridicule as a drunk, he only told his story when several other prominent citizens told of similar experiences. It seems that this strange creature had actually been seen as early as 1862. Judge Lemuel Standifer saw the creature near Rome, Georgia. The famed riverboat captain James M. Elliott also reported seeing a strange creature drifting slowly near Rome.

Reported sightings of this creature would emerge over the next several years from Rome to Wills Creek just below Gadsden. Each sighting told of a large serpent-like monster about 15 to 20 feet long and covered with scales and large fins. It would always disappear beneath the water when anyone attempted to get close to it. A group of people rafting down the river reported seeing the same creature about 2 miles below Gadsden. Each time the monster was reported, it was seen for only a few minutes and then would disappear beneath the water.

An explanation for the appearance of the creature was given in 1882. A newspaper reporter saw a great disturbance in the water and he attempted to get a closer look. An up-close investigation revealed a large clump of leaves and weeds thrown up from the bottom by an accumulation of gases beneath. Most people living along the banks of the Coosa River accepted this theory, and the strange river monster of the Coosa River was never reported again.

Steamboats were also constructed at Gadsden, although most boats were built at Rome. Captain James M. Elliott Jr. founded the Gadsden Steamboat Company, which assembled and launched several steamboats, including the *City of Gadsden* and the *Coosawattee*. Another boat, named the *Hercules*, was constructed by Colonel R.B. Kyle to haul logs to his sawmill located at Gadsden. A total of at least 40 riverboats plied the waters of this river during these years.

Another great resource that the riverboats transported between Gadsden and Rome were the hundreds and hundreds of tourists. Noccalula Falls was a favorite attraction of

This 1887 view shows the property owned by Colonel R.B. Kyle. The buildings marked with a "K" indicate some of Kyle's holdings.

The Bellevue Hotel, built in 1889, was one of Gadsden's early landmarks. This huge structure also housed the Mineral Springs Hotel and the Jones College for Young Ladies.

tourists who made the excursion to Gadsden and were then transported to the falls by horse-drawn carriage and wagon. An evening of picnicking and dancing at the pavilion located beneath the falls was a popular outing. This dance pavilion was a local favorite as early as the 1870s. By midnight, the weary travelers were transported back to the riverboat landing for the trip back to Rome the following morning.

While the riverboat traffic brought commerce and trade, there were several other early industries that were important to the Gadsden area during the days following the Civil War. Colonel R.B. Kyle brought several of these industries to the city and amassed a large fortune during this time. Kyle operated a large lumber mill on the banks of the Coosa River near the present site of the Meighan Bridge. This sawmill cut hundreds of feet of timber each day and supplied large quantities of timber during the days of the city's rapid growth.

Other Gadsden industries in which Kyle was quite active during this period included the building of the first railroad from Gadsden to Attalla. Colonel Kyle and W.P. Hollingsworth worked together on this early railroad project. In 1887, Colonel Kyle founded the Gadsden Furnace Company near the bank of the Coosa River in North Gadsden. This furnace was at one time the largest coke furnace in the South.

Another business that Kyle was instrumental in founding was the Gadsden Land and Improvement Company, also in 1887. This company was important in the real estate market in Gadsden and the surrounding area. The Gadsden Land and Improvement Company built the famous Bellevue Hotel on the brow of Lookout Mountain in 1889. Although the hotel remained in an unfinished state for several years, it would become one of Gadsden's early recognizable landmarks. This hotel was built at a cost of $35,000 and contained 72 spacious rooms. Huge bedrooms, elegant dining rooms, several parlors, and a massive ballroom brought many people to visit Lookout Mountain during this period.

Another industry that was important to Gadsden was the Elliott Car Works, originally founded by by Captain James M. Elliott Jr., Colonel R.B. Kyle, Thomas "Stonewall" Kyle, and Marcus L. Foster in 1887. This industry was established to construct and repair railroad cars, and Captain Elliott soon turned it into Gadsden's largest employer. During its early days, the Elliott Car Works had the capability of producing 15 boxcars per day. Elliott brought in the most highly skilled workers available, and the railroad cars they produced were sent throughout the United States. The car works employed more than 350 employees during the height of production.

With the coming of the Elliott Car Works, a chapter in Gadsden's history came to a close. The area located near the car works, known simply as "Pulltight," had actually come into existence during the late 1870s with the arrival of the railroads. This area was a community of saloons, disorderly houses, and gambling establishments where illegal whiskey flowed freely and the small Gadsden police force would not even attempt to enforce the laws. At this time, the city had a police department of 23 officers, 21 of whom were volunteers.

Probably the worst period of Pulltight's long history was between 1882 and 1885, when Etowah County was placed under the prohibition law passed by the state legislature without a vote by the citizens. This was probably the most lawless period in Gadsden's history. The small volunteer band of Gadsden's police department made many spectacular raids on several blind tigers—illegal drinking establishments—operating in the Gadsden area at this time.

The Gadsden Car Works was founded as the Elliott Car Works in 1887. This plant built and repaired railroad cars and employed over 350 people.

The Elliott Car Works could turn out up to 50 railroad cars a day at the height of production. The car works was located on North Twelfth Street at the foot of Lookout Mountain.

Pulltight was popular with the railroad workers, who found these businesses much to their liking. Most of these workers were rough, tough individuals who drove scrapers and wielded picks and shovels. They shot craps on the ground and on the store porches and played cards out in the open without being bothered by city or county officials. They could get all the wildcat whiskey they wanted here.

Eventually, the public outcry became so great and so much pressure was put on the Gadsden Police Department that frequent raids were carried out against the places of business in Pulltight. After a period of time, this area began to slowly fade and these establishments closed. By 1887, Pulltight was practically non-existent.

It was also during these years that the city of Gadsden lost its first police officer in the line of duty. By the year 1888, a marshal and deputy marshal were elected by the city council. A small police force was also employed at the rate of $24 per month. One such officer was D.J. Kinney, who had moved to Gadsden from Rome in 1887. He worked as a carpenter for a year before joining the police force, where he quickly proved to be an efficient officer, always at his post of duty, and a strictly sober Christian gentleman.

On November 12, 1888, a Monday morning, Deputy Marshal D.J. Kinney and John Cunningham went to a small, two-room house for the purpose of arresting a suspect believed to be hiding there. Kinney went to the front door and Cunningham went to the back door to prevent an escape. Kinney pushed the door open and stepped inside. As he did, Charley Johnson, alias Charley Holmes, stepped from behind the door with a gun in his hand and ordered Kinney to leave or he would kill him. As Kinney was turning to leave, Johnson fired.

When Cunningham heard the shot, he pushed open the back door and attempted to fire, but his pistol failed to work. Johnson then told Cunningham to leave or he would kill him, too. Cunningham dove out the back door as Kinney staggered out the front door with blood streaming down his side. Kinney was picked up and carried to a nearby residence where a doctor was summoned. All possible medical attention was given, but D.J. Kinney breathed his last about noon.

Johnson fled to the mountains following the shooting. The citizens of Gadsden were aroused by the murder, and a large mob soon formed in hot pursuit of the suspect, searching the mountain for miles yet unable to locate the murderer. Mayor John Disque telegraphed to Rising Fawn, Georgia, for bloodhounds to aid in the search. A reward of $200 was placed on the head of the suspect payable to anyone who could bring him back to Gadsden to stand trial for the killing of the police officer.

The case remained unsolved until a former Gadsden resident working in a small Tennessee town recognized Johnson. John Lindsey knew of the tragic murder and got in touch with Gadsden officers, who went and picked up the suspect. He was brought back to Gadsden, tried, and hanged.

Although Gadsden was still a town of dirt roads, horse-drawn wagons, and wooden storefronts during the early 1880s, the growing village soon took its first real step toward providing for the cultural arts. A small theater, known as Dramatic Hall, had been in operation during the 1870s. This small wooden building was constructed like a Greek temple, and it paved the way for the first opera house to open in Gadsden in 1881.

Colonel R.B. Kyle had long hoped to bring a large theater to downtown Gadsden. His plans were to build and operate a theater that would rival the theaters of larger cities throughout the Southeast. The property Kyle chose was in the 400 block of Broad Street, and was purchased from James Moragne for $300 on May 11, 1880.

Kyle set out to turn this property into Kyle's Opera House. He brought in the finest carpenters, brick masons, and craftsmen to carry out his plans. The building housed the Lowenthall and Hersteig Store on the first floor and would house Kyle's Opera House on the second and third floors. The finest lumber came from Kyle's sawmill for the interior of the opera house. The structure was built of brick like the Kyle building next door, which was the first brick building erected on Broad Street.

The opera house was completed in November 1881. The theater was lighted with carbide gas that was also used in lighting the store underneath and also the adjoining stores of R.B. Kyle. There were no boxes in Kyle's Opera House, but there were modern opera chairs downstairs. The gallery upstairs had wooden benches with a low wall separating white and black patrons. The main entrance was in the center of the building with a steep flight of stairs leading to the main doors.

Reserved seats were sold from a box sheet at the one-price store beneath the theater. The sheet was made from a drawing of the main auditorium with numbers for each seat. The sheet was fastened to a soft-pine board and, as tickets sold, a tack was pressed through the seat number on the board to indicate that it had been reserved. The corresponding numbers were written on the tickets. The board rested on top of a showcase in front so that it could be inspected by anyone. The store served as the box office.

Just before the theater opened, Marcus Foster, the manager, would call for the board and the leftover tickets and then open the regular box office upstairs. Most tickets were sold there.

Gadsden was still a town of wooden store fronts and dirt roads when R.B. Kyle built Kyle's Opera House in the 400 block of Broad Street. The opera house is the large three-story brick building in the middle of the block.

The grand opening of Kyle's Opera House was set for November 29, 1881. A special engagement was booked starring the great English artist Clarie Scott, supported by S.K. Coburn and a company of New York and London artists. The grand inaugural consisted of Victor Hugo's masterpiece, *Lucretia Borgia*. Patrons paid $1 for reserved seats, while general admission was 75¢. Gallery seating was 50¢. A capacity crowd of 1,100 people turned out for the grand opening.

The Gadsden City Council issued a proclamation commending Kyle for his contribution to the city and granted him a one-year exemption of taxes on his beautiful opera house. Kyle's Opera House booked many fine attractions that found it convenient to fill in between other engagements in Birmingham and Chattanooga. For many years, quality programs were presented at this theater, including operas, concerts, dramas, and school programs.

Many great political leaders of the day also spoke at Kyle's Opera House. Colonel Rattray of Cherokee County, one of the most respected Democrats in this area, delivered a speech on behalf of democracy at 11 o'clock that lasted until 1 o'clock without tiring anyone. This business venture of Colonel R.B. Kyle's was by far his favorite. Although hundreds of hours were spent at the opera house by many of the residents of Gadsden, the greatest single contribution of this brick theater came on July 4, 1883.

Independence Day was one holiday that was celebrated with many patriotic events in Gadsden. The July 4, 1883 celebration was to be centered around a horse-swapper

George Christopher (left) and George Woodliff (right) are shown here in their Etowah Rifles uniforms. This local militia group aided in fighting a destructive fire on July 4, 1883, when much of downtown Gadsden burned. The Etowah Rifles stood guard later to prevent looting.

convention that had brought several hundred visitors to the city. After the horses were displayed, the "Etowah Rifles" staged a colorful military parade, which ended at the courthouse. This local militia group was formed in 1883, with Judge John H. Disque as its first captain. The group originally consisted of many Confederate veterans and young men seeking to give something back to the community. Under the leadership of Disque, the Etowah Rifles were frequently called out to quell disturbances throughout the county and elsewhere in the state. The colorful, showy organization also won its share of prizes in annual competitions and was very popular at home.

Following the parade staged by the Etowah Rifles, a speech was given at the Etowah County Courthouse by Colonel William H. Denson. About one hour into the address, the calm was broken by the sounding of the fire alarm. As people ran to get the firefighting equipment, thick, black smoke was seen billowing from the direction of the Ben Whorton residence on the corner of Third and Broad Streets.

At this time, Gadsden had only a small bucket brigade that was manned by a volunteer force. There was an unusually brisk wind blowing from the east to the west, which quickly caused the fire to spread. Store owners frantically attempted to remove goods from their places of business, but the intoxicated horse swappers removed the goods as fast as they were brought to the street.

The flames spread from building to building until the fire had reached the end of the block, crossing Fourth Street and burning on toward Kyle's Opera House. The Gadsden Fire Department, aided by the Etowah Rifles, fought gallantly, but 26 businesses were destroyed before the fire burned itself out against the fireproof brick walls of the opera house.

Gadsden's fire department was a small unit of only 40 volunteers. Water to fight this major fire was transported by buckets from the well near the courthouse on Broad Street. Estimates of the damage ran as high as $100,000. The firefighters fought the blaze into the late hours of the night, with the Etowah Rifles standing guard to prevent looting and pilfering.

The fire was a major setback for downtown Gadsden. It had nearly destroyed two city blocks in the main business district and heavily damaged the new telephone company, which had only recently opened. Two years later, this burned-out area had been completely rebuilt with new brick structures, many of which still stand today.

Gadsden made its first attempt at a rapid transit system during 1886, when a street railway system was started. Colonel R.B. Kyle, Herman Herzberg, and their associates petitioned the Gadsden City Council to grant the Gadsden Land and Improvement Company a franchise to build a horse-drawn street railroad in Gadsden. Kyle named the company the Gadsden Streetcar Company.

Streetcars were a way of life in the Gadsden area from their beginnings in 1887 until the time they were discontinued in 1934. The electric cars ran from Gadsden to Alabama City and on to Attalla.

The tracks ran from Fourth and Locust Streets to Broad Street, then to Firth Street, south to Walnut Street to Forrest Avenue, and then to Ninth Street. In 1887, the first streetcar pulled by mules went into operation. These early mule-drawn streetcars were very slow and the trip to downtown Gadsden took quite some time. A story was told about a young lady who was waiting to catch the streetcar to downtown when she decided to go inside and change her dress just as the car was pulling up. After a while, she returned to find the car still waiting for her at the stop. Business was slow during these days and the driver did not want to miss this nickel fare.

The streetcars were changed in 1888 from mule-drawn cars to a steam dummy line. A small steam locomotive was enclosed in a rectangular box and pulled the passenger coaches. With the addition of these steam engines, the street railway became a more popular and faster mode of transportation. A major event took place in February 1890 in the life of the streetcar line when the Gadsden Land and Improvement Company authorized the sale of the dummy line to Captain James M. Elliott Jr.

Another unusual feature of downtown Gadsden was the block known as "Tunnel Block." This part of Broad Street that grew up in the late 1860s and early 1870s was a group of wooden storefronts located in the 500 and 600 block. The eight store buildings on the north side of the 500 block became known simply as Tunnel Block because they were built over a large depression in that section that was caused by erosion.This ravine actually ran from Chestnut Street to Locust Street.

Several of the stores in Tunnel Block were two-story buildings, with the second floor at the present sidewalk level of Broad Street. The lower floor of these stores was below ground level. A long boardwalk served the second stories as a sidewalk. The ravine where these businesses were located was so deep that a person on the lower end of Broad Street could not see a wagon in the ravine of Tunnel Block.

Some of the leading businesses in downtown Gadsden were once located there. One of the more popular stores was Paden Brother's General Merchandise, which dealt in the finest leather goods of the day. John C. Paden, one member of this firm, went on to become one of the wealthiest businessmen of Gadsden. He later constructed a three-story building on Fourth Street just south of the Printup Hotel and opened the Paden-Ewing Hardware Company. Some of the other stores included the Henry Woodward Dry Goods Store and a store operated by John T. Martin. A large brick livery stable near the middle of the block was operated by B.A. Kyle. This building was later used as an icehouse.

A major problem with these storehouses was flooding. Heavy rains caused the ravine to fill with water, flooding the bottom stories of buildings. The problem became worse each year, and eventually the bottom floors were abandoned. On more than one occasion, a flash flood caused trapped livestock to drown in the rising water. A flatbottom boat was kept tied up at Chestnut and Sixth Streets to be used when this area flooded.

When the bottom floors were abandoned because of the water, the whole block began to deteriorate and it became a real eyesore. Eventually the weather boarding was removed from the lower buildings and the upper stores were propped up by pine poles.

John Potter and James Bailey once taught a school in one of these buildings. At least one of these structures housed a blind tiger, and a disorderly house—the polite name for a brothel—occupied another.

The Paden-Ewing Hardware Company was located on North Fourth Street. This store was a favorite spot for people to gather on Saturday mornings.

While several problem areas, such as the Tunnel Block, existed in Gadsden during the late 1880s, the small town was also experiencing general growing pains. It was during 1888 that the first bridge was built across the Coosa River at Gadsden. This railroad trestle would serve for many years as the only way for pedestrians as well as horses and buggies or wagons to cross the river. A gateman was stationed on each side of the river to regulate pedestrian traffic and to warn of oncoming locomotives. Before the construction of this bridge, the only way to cross the waterway was by using one of the many ferries located up and down the river.

Ferryboats were used to transport goods, horses, wagons, and people across the river. A ferry was a large boat attached to a cable that was stretched across the river. The ferry would transport travelers across the river for a fare. The first ferry to operate across the Coosa River at Gadsden was known as Walker's Ferry; it was later known as the Ewing Ferry, with its landing on the west bank of the river at the present site of Coosa Street. It was on the original stage line from Jacksonville to Huntsville. There were several other ferries operating in the Gadsden area in the years before the construction of the first bridge across the Coosa River, but the ferries soon began to vanish with the construction of other bridges over the years.

Another big news story of 1888 was the construction of Gadsden's beautiful Printup Hotel, which opened on July 4, 1888. This imposing four-story structure was built on the corner of Fourth and Locust Streets in downtown Gadsden. This hotel was Gadsden's

Gadsden's Printup Hotel opened on July 4, 1888. This imposing four-story structure was built on the corner of Fourth and Locusts Streets in downtown Gadsden and was furnished at a cost of $18,000.

first large hotel and was the scene of many important meetings during the late 1880s. The Printup was elaborately furnished at a cost of $18,000, an unheard of amount during the late 1800s.

By the early days of 1890, Gadsden was growing in every direction. Industry was beginning to locate to the area and more people were moving to the city. A small business district that once was lined with wooden storefronts now boasted beautiful brick buildings. The small town that had survived the Civil War was incorporated in 1871 and began to grow at a rapid rate. Under the able leadership of people such as Judge John H. Disque, Colonel R.B. Kyle, Captain James M. Elliott Jr., and General D.C. Turrentine, the small village that began as a dream of Gabriel Hughes, John S. Moragne, and Joseph Hughes soon became an important town in northeast Alabama. Moving into the 1890s, Gadsden experienced another period of accelerated growth and greater prosperity.

5. Alabama City and the 1890s

The 1890s were an important decade in the growth of the city of Gadsden. Several events took place that would have far-reaching effects on this small city that was struggling to become an industrial center in North Alabama. Two of Gadsden's leading businesses and civic leaders once again worked together in a joint endeavor of a different kind to bring industry to the Gadsden area, and their efforts brought a new town into existence. This new town became an industrial area and eventually extended the city limits of Gadsden to Attalla.

Captain James M. Elliott Jr. had become a resident of Gadsden and opened several major businesses in the area. The Elliott Peach Orchard, located at the present site of the Gadsden Country Club, was canning and shipping peaches throughout the United States. Riverboat production was underway on the banks of the Coosa River under the careful supervision of Captain Elliott, and hundreds of railroad cars were being produced at the Elliott Car Works. The Elliott Car Works was growing at such a rate that Elliott was planning to use this business to form a new town.

With the help of his father-in-law, Colonel R.B. Kyle, Captain Elliott began to draw up plans for a new town about 2 miles west of Gadsden. The dream of Elliott was to develop this new town as an industrial center and eventually merge this town with Gadsden and Attalla into one major city. The town became a reality in 1890 when Captain Elliott, Colonel R.B. Kyle, and T.S. Kyle met to found Alabama City.

At the time of its founding, Alabama City was a very sparsely settled area—not the large industrial development that Captain Elliott had envisioned. Several families did live in this area, and the small store of Frank Canterberry was also situated here, although very little else was located in the new town. The town grew slowly at first, although early the following year, Captain Elliott filed for incorporation, and a charter was granted to Elliott for his city in 1891.

Captain Elliott applied for a post office for the new village in 1891. A post office was granted, and Captain Elliott directed the mail from the car works through the Alabama City post office in order to pay the first postmaster, J.K. Fleming. This large volume of mail gave this new post office a substantial amount of business during its early days. The first elections were held for Alabama City in March 1891, and William Gardner was elected the town's first mayor.

Captain James M. Elliott Jr., along with Colonel R.B. Kyle, founded Alabama City as an industrial center between Gadsden and Attalla in 1890. The new city was incorporated in 1891.

The first major industry to locate in Alabama City was the Kyle Furniture Company in 1891. This manufacturing plant was located on the banks of Black Creek and was to make hand-carved tables. Colonel R.B. Kyle founded the company and built the plant in Alabama City to give the small village a "shot in the arm" and attract new citizens to the town. Kyle attempted to bring the finest craftsmen available to Alabama City, and a fine-quality product was produced at his small factory. These beautiful tables became popular, and they were shipped throughout the United States. But a major mistake was made in the location of this factory because of the fact that Black Creek was prone to flooding during the months of spring. A major flood did occur on Black Creek that did considerable damage to the Kyle Furniture Company. Colonel Kyle made plans to relocate his plant and continue the production of these tables, although the plans were never fulfilled and the plant never reopened. Although this first industry was in existence for only a short time, it paved the way for another major industry that relocated to Alabama City a few short years later.

During the year 1890, the streetcar line in Gadsden was extended through the new village of Alabama City and on to Attalla. Captain Elliott, who had recently purchased the streetcar line, had agreed to extend the tracks through his new town and on to the passenger station at the junction of the railroads in Attalla. Rails were laid and 750 telephone poles were acquired to extend the newly electrified streetcar line to Alabama City and Attalla—this played a major role in linking Gadsden and Alabama City. From 1891 to 1895, Alabama City grew at a slow pace until an announcement was made that brought drastic changes to this small town.

One of the earliest businesses in Alabama City was the store of Frank Canterberry. Later Colonel R.B. Kyle opened the Alabama City Furniture Company as the young town's first industry.

A large work force came to the small town of Alabama City when the Dwight Manufacturing Company announced that it would build a large cotton mill in town.

This photograph shows the early construction of the Dwight Manufacturing Company. This mill would grow to over 957,000 square feet with several later additions.

Colonel R.B. Kyle worked tirelessly to bring another major industry to the Alabama City area for the next few years. His effort was rewarded in 1895 when an announcement was made by the Dwight Manufacturing Company of Chicopee, Massachusetts, that a large cotton mill would be located in this town. The company sent officials to the 3,000-acre town to begin plans to bring this industry to Etowah County. Colonel Kyle offered to donate the land to build this textile plant.

A large workforce of carpenters, brick masons, and skilled craftsmen were sent to Alabama City to begin construction on the mill and mill village immediately. The mill was constructed of brick on a large parcel of land that was known as "Dwight City," which would eventually become part of Alabama City. A large mill village was also constructed to house the hundreds of workers that were needed to operate the textile giant. The mill village fanned out from the mill like the spokes of a giant wheel. The handsome cottages ranged from three to six rooms and rented for $1 per month per room.

Every comfort was taken in laying out the mill village. The yards around the cottages were large, and a place was provided for a garden at each house. Each home was given an identity of its own, making the residences enjoyable for the people who would be spending long hours in the mill.

The army of construction workers converged on Alabama City following the announcement of the coming of the Dwight Mill. Within a few short months of the beginning of construction, several hundred houses had been raised, the main structure of the Dwight Manufacturing Company was nearing completion, and the most recognizable three homes in Alabama City had been built.

This beautiful mill agent's home, along with the school superintendent's house and company doctor's home, are located on Hillcrest Avenue.

Workers' cottages were rented at a rate of $1 per room per month. The standard of living for employees of the Dwight Manufacturing Company was quite high.

During the days of construction, three grand homes were built by the mill carpenters from the Dwight Manufacturing Company. These houses were erected on a large hill overlooking the mill village and cotton mill below. The street became known as Hillcrest Avenue, or simply "Boss Hill" to many of the people living in Alabama City. The three homes were for the company doctor, the mill agent, and the school superintendent.

Entering Boss Hill from Cabot Avenue, the company doctor's home was the first house on the left. Containing spacious rooms with 12-foot ceilings, each home had a large wrap-around porch, oak floors, and walls of plaster. The mill agent's home was the large house in the middle. A two-story home complete with a gingerbread gazebo, it was the centerpiece of these grand homes. The third house was built to be occupied by the school superintendent of Alabama City. Much like the company doctor's home, the house has a spacious central hall with assorted living spaces. Oak mantels with beveled mirrors and columns, adorned by hand-carvings, added to the overall beauty.

As the construction of the cotton mill and mill village was nearing completion, the Dwight Company began to recruit skilled laborers throughout the Southeast. The mill village began to draw more and more people to Alabama City seeking employment and a higher standard of living. The opening of the textile mill saw the population of the small village begin to grow at a steady pace.

Construction nears completion in this photo taken from the rear of the mill, near the present location of Coolidge Circle.

The Union Church was provided by the Dwight Manufacturing Company to be used by all denominations on a rotating basis.

One of the major factors in the growth of the town and the cotton mill was a dynamic individual who came to Alabama City from Massachusetts, an energetic 24-year-old man named Howard Gardner Nichols. Nichols recognized the natural beauty of Alabama City and the splendor of nearby Noccalula Falls. In his letters home to his parents, he told of the great natural resources of Lookout Mountain, Alabama City, and Gadsden. Nichols was a tireless worker in both his job with the Dwight Manufacturing Company, which was owned by his family, as well as civic work in the town of Alabama City. Nichols served this town as one of its early mayors.

Howard Gardner Nichols was an energetic and indefatigable worker at the cotton mill. While he was helping to move a large piece of machinery in May 1896, a large dynamo fell and seriously injured the young Nichols, who was aiding construction workers. The heavy machinery trapped Nichols underneath. Doctors were summoned, although they gave little hope because of the seriousness of the injuries. Nichols was transferred to an Atlanta hospital where he underwent surgery for internal injuries. For a short while, it appeared that Nichols would recover; however, he took a turn for the worse and passed away on June 23, 1896. A stunned Alabama City paid their last respects to a young man who had helped their small town to grow quickly in a very short time.

For the many people who relocated to Alabama City to work in the cotton mill during these early years, work was hard and the hours were long. Child labor was also used at the mill and the pay was small. Even though the working conditions were extreme, at times, the company attempted to provide for the comfort of its employees in every way possible. Not only were living conditions good in the new homes of the mill village, but the company attempted to provide other comforts for the mill workers, as well.

One basic need that the company attempted to meet was the spiritual need of its employees. During the early days of the cotton mill, church was actually held inside the mill on Sunday mornings. The first congregation established at the cotton mill was the Dwight Baptist Church, which was organized on October 3, 1897, making it the oldest church in Alabama City. The first church structure erected in Alabama City was the Union Church, built in 1900 at a cost of $6,000. This church was intended for all religious denominations, which shared the building by alternating weeks. Dwight Baptist Church was growing quickly, and its congregation soon outgrew the building of the Union Church. Plans were quickly drawn up for the congregation's first church building. This church, located at the corner of Waters and Summersworth Avenues, was completed in March 1901, with the dedication being held on September 29, 1901.

Other attempts were made to meet the needs of the mill workers. The mill company provided social functions, sporting events, band concerts, and a large lake, complete with a bathhouse, at the back of the mill. The large spring-fed lake was a favorite spot for many of the mill workers during the hot days of summer. The bathhouse located at the east end of the lake was ideal for swimming and enjoying the cold water of the lake.

Dwight Manufacturing Company, like many of the other cotton mills located throughout the Southeast, provided a company baseball team. This team was known as

A large spring-fed lake and bathhouse were located at the back of the cotton mill.

A large bandstand was provided by the company for the enjoyment of its employees.

the "Dwights" and was very competitive on the baseball diamond. An exceptional athlete did not have a problem finding a job at the local mill if he was willing to display his talent on the diamond. Although these teams were not considered professionals, people took these games very seriously and a good ballplayer was known throughout the city. The Dwights played at Dwight Park, which was located on the banks of Black Creek. This ballpark was small during its early years and had a wooden grandstand and wooden bleachers. In later years, the park was enlarged and was the site of many baseball games as well as many of the early high school football games played in this area.

The company also provided a large bandstand located in a shady grove of trees near the mill. This bandstand was the scene of many great Sunday afternoon concerts that featured the mill's brass band as well as many visiting high school bands.

Alabama City was also the site of the first free public lending library in the state of Alabama. This small library was erected by the Dwight Manufacturing Company in memory of Howard Gardner Nichols, the son of Howard and Charlotte Nichols of Massachusetts. The library opened in the spring of 1900 as a lasting memorial to young Nichols. The library was supplied with over 2,500 books, including educational, historical, and standard works of famous authors. It also offered the best books for children and the latest fiction. Also, all lending magazines and local daily newspapers were available to library patrons. The library was free and was open every evening from 7:00 to 9:00 and between 1:00 and 3:00 on Sunday afternoons.

As the small town of Alabama City began to attract more and more residents, businesses began to locate to the area as well. One business that opened here in early 1900 was the Dwight Inn, the first and only hotel built in Alabama City. The inn was a beautiful wooden structure on Dwight Square across from the main entrance to the mill. The inn, or "boarding house" as it was also called, had 20 well-furnished rooms. A room could be rented for $2.50 per week. A major fire broke out at the Dwight Inn on September 1, 1900, causing heavy damage, but owner J.A. Pettigrew rebuilt the hotel and re-opened it a short time later. Known for its beauty, the Dwight Inn continued to be a landmark in Alabama City for many years to come.

In the early part of the twentieth century, Alabama City was growing at a rapid rate. Later additions to the cotton mill brought more and more jobs to the area. With the growth of the small town's population, more businesses also relocated to the mill village.

Alabama City was founded to bring industry to the Gadsden area. Captain James M. Elliott Jr.'s dream was to eventually merge Gadsden, Alabama City, and Attalla into one large city. With the coming of the Dwight Manufacturing Company, Captain Elliott soon set about the task of planning to merge the three towns. He envisioned a city of more than

Etowah County's new courthouse was built on the site of the first structure in 1890. This imposing building was dedicated on October 25, 1890.

1 million people in the not-so-distant future, and he worked on this task the remaining years of his life.

The 1890s saw the city of Gadsden also growing at a fast pace. Several new businesses opened in downtown and new industry also located to Gadsden. Education began to reach a new level, with the first school board being formed and a new college moving to the Gadsden area.

By the early 1890s, the original Etowah County Courthouse was beginning to show its age; it was also too small to house the many county offices. The question was also brought up whether to keep the county seat in Gadsden or move it to Attalla. To cloud matters even more, Attalla offered to build a new courthouse at no cost to the county if the county seat would be moved. A committee of five convened to discuss and vote on the matter. Commissioners J.B. Washburn and E.A. Gilliland voted to move the seat of county government to Attalla. Commissioners John Miller and Dan G. McCurley voted to retain it in Gadsden. Probate Judge James A. Tallman, the official chairman, broke the tie by voting to keep it in Gadsden. Plans were made following this decision to build a new courthouse in Gadsden.

The new Etowah County Courthouse was built on the same property as the original structure. This new building, however, was constructed closer to Broad Street rather than Locust Street. The brick courthouse was completed in the late fall and dedicated on October 25, 1890. The cost of this new structure, trimmed in blue granite, was $70,000. The most impressive feature of the courthouse was the 126-foot-high clock tower.

The building was accessible by two winding stairways in the front and one in the rear. A small park was located behind the courthouse, complete with a beautiful fountain and overhanging trees, making it an ideal place to relax and visit. Ice cream festivals and strawberry festivals were often held here under the shade trees.

During the decade of the 1890s, John Flynn and William Hagen built the first cast-iron soil pipe foundry in Gadsden. This foundry was located downtown at the corner of Second and Broad Streets. The foundry was later taken over by William H. Weller and was renamed the Weller Pipe Works.

An event took place at a carnival during the 1890s that soon brought about a drastic change in the way people would go to the theater. For many years, Kyle's Opera House had been the center of the social life in downtown Gadsden. Live productions, operas, and musicals were performed on the stage there almost weekly, but the citizens of Gadsden were introduced to a new type of entertainment at a traveling carnival on Locust Street during the mid-1890s. Moving pictures soon proved to be more than a passing fad and quickly replaced the live show as the most popular form of entertainment. Although the first moving picture, or electric, theater was still several years away, the moving picture had definitely made its mark on the people of Gadsden.

In the 1890s, Gadsden also made great strides in the field of public education. A legislative act adopted on February 18, 1895, provided for the appointment of five citizens of Gadsden to a board of education. This first Gadsden Board of Education was composed of Judge John H. Disque (chairman), Colonel R.B. Kyle, J.M. Moragne, W.G. Brockway, and Amos B. Goodhue. Judge Disque dedicated much of the remaining years of his life to improving the level of public education in Gadsden.

The year 1895 saw another major story dealing with education on the local scene. This involved the beautiful Bellevue Hotel, located on the brow of Lookout Mountain, that had closed in 1894 following the financial panic of 1893–1894. The hotel remained closed until 1895, when it was purchased by Reverend A.B. Jones of Huntsville. Jones was the founder of the Huntsville Female College. This popular Huntsville school had suffered a destructive fire in January 1895, reducing the school's facilities to ashes. Reverend Jones visited many points in several states before settling on the former Bellevue Hotel in which to reopen his college. This location was chosen because of its accessibility to the railroads and the facilities that were readily available. A total of 135 students from several states attended the Jones College for Young Ladies during its first term in 1895.

The old hotel's 72 rooms were ideal for a college, with spacious rooms, a large dining hall, and elegant ballroom. Although this hotel had been in an unfinished state for several years, Reverend Jones spared little expense in completing the beautiful building. An extensive course of study was offered at the Jones College, including art, music, and several foreign languages. Young ladies attending the college were required to dress appropriately and were not allowed to go to downtown Gadsden without a member of the faculty along as a chaperon.

Several prominent Gadsden residents served on the board of trustees of the Jones College during its only year of operation. Colonel R.B. Kyle, Captain James M. Elliott Jr., Captain J.T. Brooks, John Burnett, E.T. Hollingsworth, and professor J.W. Dubose all served on this board. The operation of the college was administered by Reverend and Mrs. A.B. Jones.

The Jones College for Young Ladies was advertised throughout the Southeast, and students did attend from several states, including Texas and North Dakota. Although the college appeared to be a popular one, Reverend Jones experienced financial problems during this first year, and the college was eventually forced to close. This early college had, however, made its mark on Gadsden. The Bellevue Hotel property was placed on the market once again, and once again it was reopened as a hotel. The building was enlarged and the hotel welcomed guests to the scenic beauty of Lookout Mountain. This grand hotel flourished in the years leading into the twentieth century.

Another first was introduced to the Gadsden area during the 1890s. On February 26, 1897, sports fans in Gadsden watched their first match of the new sport of football. This game was played at the athletic field in Gadsden between the Gadsden Athletic Club and the Athletic Club of Montgomery.

The early football contest was played in unfavorable weather conditions, and the field was almost unplayable. There were occasional showers on the day of the game, and the day before had seen heavy rain—the field was almost swimming in water when the teams lined up. The southern half of the field was soggy and pools of water stood elsewhere. It was almost impossible to make a run of any sort, and when the ball reached the muddy territory, it stayed right there, with neither team able to kick it out. During the second half of the game, there was a steady downpour.

Despite the conditions, the local team played a splendid game. Montgomery had the larger and stronger team, although Gadsden made up for this with speed at the ends. The

Montgomery Club seemed afraid to attempt to run around the end, choosing to run the center of the Gadsden line. Montgomery's running game was held in check for much of the game, and its deepest penetration was a long kick by the fullback. Captain Charles Wood and Snow Perkins made several long gains for the Gadsden squad, although they were unable to cross the goal.

The stands were fairly well filled considering the rainy weather. Hometown pride was evident as ribbons of white and purple, the colors of the Gadsden team, were worn by many of the fans. The colors of the Montgomery team, gold and white, also were scattered throughout the spectators. The sponsors of the two teams, Mrs. Louis Herzberg and Miss Buena Vista Riley (for Gadsden) and Misses Eula Duncan and Leila Fletcher (for the visitors), were out to lend encouragement to the young warriors. Will Hight of Anniston was referee, Louis Herzberg, the umpire, and Tom McHan, the lineman.

Gadsden won the toss and chose the goal. A player named Seibels kicked off for Montgomery. Ed Hughes fielded the kick and returned it 10 yards to the 20-yard line. On second down, Wood broke loose on a 10-yard run. Two plays later Gadsden fumbled. Montgomery was unable to move the ball and Gadsden took over on downs.

Louis Herzberg served as the umpire for the first football game between the Gadsden Athletic Club and the Montgomery Athletic Club. Herzberg played a major role in bringing the game to Gadsden.

The game was mainly a defensive struggle for the remainder of the first half, with neither team threatening to cross the other's goal. The steady rain caused each team to play a conservative game. As the gun sounded to end the first half, it was obvious to those who remained in the grandstand that they were quickly becoming fans of this new sport.

The second half was a defensive struggle as well. On two occasions, it appeared Gadsden would cross the goal line. Perkins, the left halfback for Gadsden, took the ball around right end for a 15-yard gain. He fell in the mud after getting behind the Montgomery team. Later Charles Wood, the Gadsden right halfback, broke loose on a long run only to be pulled down from behind.

Montgomery came close to scoring when it kicked the ball over the Gadsden goal. A player named Davis fielded the kick and kicked the ball back out. Gadsden's defense held, taking over on downs. Neither team made any material gains in the next few plays and the time-keeper called the game with the ball deep in Gadsden's territory. The game ended with the score standing at 0 to 0.

Other "games" had taken the Gadsden area by storm during the late 1890s. These games were chess, checkers, and backgammon, and they were played by young and old alike. A favorite place for local players to meet was Professor J.W. DuBose's Book Store in downtown Gadsden. Many amateurs came here to challenge DuBose in chess, a game in which he was considered an expert. He was invited to play in many state tournaments, and he was rarely defeated.

With the popularity of these games rapidly growing, an amazing individual emerged in the person of C.B. Cross. Known by many as Charlie Betty Cross to distinguish him from Charles F. Cross, the jeweler, this young lawyer had an uncanny ability at checkers.

Cross was able to work out all possible moves in advance and could play for months at a time without losing a single game. Amateurs and professionals alike came to Gadsden to try their hand against the young lawyer. Each person who came met the same fate—Cross emerged victorious. These matches were played at a very fast pace, and Cross never hesitated about a move. Cross took on all comers and played in every tournament that was available, winning time after time. Tournament players came to Gadsden and he beat everyone without exception. For several years, Cross met each challenge with the same success and was considered the greatest checker player in the United States. He was so successful that many of his friends tried to get him to try his hand at chess, although he was not interested and was only an average player. C.B. Cross later left the Gadsden area and moved to Texas to continue his law practice. He was remembered by many as a fine person, a good lawyer, and a wizard at draughts.

Gadsden grew in many ways in the 1890s. In 1893, the city had two banks, two hotels, six doctors, one bakery, one potter, five railroads, two tin shops, one shoe store, two saw mills, one car works, three dentists, two laundries, one ice plant, one pipe shop, seven law firms, two newspapers, three drugstores, one opera house, three livery stables, two millinery shops, two hardware stores, and two furniture stores. There was also one street railway owned by Captain J.M. Elliott Jr., who was extending this railway on to Alabama City and Attalla. The streetcars were also changed from the steam dummy engines to electric power. The streetcars made travel easy between the three cities of Gadsden, Alabama City, and Attalla.

The riverboats were plying the waters of the Coosa River at a record pace during the 1890s, but the river trade that had made Gadsden such an important part on the Coosa River was gradually slowing down. The railroads that had been so important to connect the rivers were now beginning to replace the steamboat as the major mode of transportation. Riverboat activities extended into the twentieth century, but it was apparent by 1890 that the peak of their use for commercial purposes had passed.

During the 1890s, Black Creek, or Noccalula Falls, was still the top tourist attraction in the Gadsden area. A beautiful covered bridge was built above the falls over Black Creek to make travel to the area easier. This covered wooden bridge was one of the early covered bridges and was a favorite place for local photographers to shoot pictures of the many people coming to enjoy the scenic beauty of the falls.

Other improvements made in Gadsden during the 1890s included those to the Gadsden Fire Department. The department that had been a small bucket brigade just a few years before welcomed, in the 1890s, the purchase of a horse-drawn steam engine by Gadsden City Council in an attempt to improve the department. The engine, pulled by a team of three horses, was used until the first motorized fire engines were purchased several years later.

Although many improvements were made during these years, there were still many problems to be addressed. Road conditions were still impassable at times during the winter and spring months following heavy rains. The construction of a city hall was still a major topic of discussion among civic leaders who were concerned that city offices were scattered throughout the downtown area. The fire department was housed in a building across Court Street from the Etowah County Courthouse. The mayor's office occupied a corner office in the courthouse and the city council held office upstairs over Mac Cummins's place of business. These problems were addressed shortly after the turn of the century when Gadsden once again enjoyed a period of rapid growth.

6. Growth into the Twentieth Century

In the early days of the twentieth century, Gadsden took on the characteristics of a much larger city. The downtown business district was lined with beautiful brick buildings, and an ornate courthouse was located on the corner of Fourth and Broad Streets. A street railway carried passengers from Attalla to Alabama City and on to Gadsden. Industry was growing in the Gadsden area with the Dwight Manufacturing Company operating at full speed and the car works turning out railroad cars at a record rate.

With this rather fast growth came many new problems. The need to construct a city hall in order to bring the many municipal offices under one roof was still felt by many of the populace. The condition of the unpaved roads was becoming more of a pressing issue with the arrival of the first automobiles to Gadsden, and a question about a new post office would soon come up. Although Gadsden faced many new challenges in the upcoming years, these problems would be met successfully one by one. This was due largely to the high-caliber people leading the city in both government and civic capacities. One such leader was a man who excelled in both the business and civic fields. This business leader, who made countless contributions to Gadsden during the early 1900s, was Mac Cummins.

Cummins was born into slavery in Talladega County in 1853. During the years following the Civil War, Cummins relocated to the Gadsden area and began to seek ways to enter the business profession. After several attempts to open his own business, Cummins opened a barbershop in the Kittrell Hotel at 119 North Fourth Street. Cummins quickly made an impact in the local community, and the barbershop was a popular establishment with many local residents. Cummins was an outstanding businessman, although he had never received a formal education. Cummins later operated a barbershop at 323 Broad Street.

During the many years of his career as a barber in Gadsden, Cummins taught many local residents the profession. For years Mac and his wife, Eugenia, contributed to the everyday life in downtown Gadsden. The Cummins family owned a home on Lister Lane and lived at this residence for most of their life. The couple was well known and respected throughout the community.

Mac Cummins moved to Gadsden and opened a barber shop in the Kittrell Hotel on North Fourth Street. He and his wife, Eugenia, also opened a restaurant at 123 North Third Street.

Of his many contributions to the Gadsden area, Mac will probably be most remembered for his business venture during the early days of the 1900s. Mac and Eugenia opened a restaurant, Mac Cummins Greenleaf Barbecue, at 123 North Third Street, and it quickly became a local favorite. The barbecue was famous for its special sauce, which contained ingredients known only to Cummins. This recipe was highly sought after for many years, although Cummins never revealed his secret.

The early days of the new century also saw the coming of the automobile, or "Tin Lizzie" as many people referred to the new horseless carriages. These vehicles brought many new benefits as well as problems to the streets of Gadsden. The early cars quickly intensified a major concern with the inadequate conditions of the roads in Gadsden. The unpaved roads had been a problem for wagons as well as with the new automobiles during the rainy days of the spring and summer months.

The automobile was first thought to be a passing fad, although more and more residents purchased them. In the early days of the automobile, the speed limit on the streets of downtown Gadsden was 5 miles per hour, but this speed limit was later raised to 8 miles per hour. The automobile quickly brought a new kind of commerce to the city. Goods could now be transported greater distances more efficiently, thus bringing citizens closer together. The early autos in the area were International Harvester motor buggies. Dr. M.P. Hughes, a prominent Gadsden physician, could be seen traveling throughout

Dr. M.P. Hughes owned one of the early automobiles in Gadsden. Exposed to the elements, Dr. Hughes often made house calls in this two-cylinder Maxwell.

These International Harvester motorbuggies were some of the earliest automobiles in Gadsden. The second Etowah County Courthouse is visible in the background.

the city making housecalls in his two-cylinder Maxwell. Hughes was also the owner of another early automobile called a Chandler.

Several of Gadsden's more prominent families also purchased new automobiles. Colonel R.B. Kyle owned a Grant, while his son T.S. Kyle drove a Packard. R.B. Kyle Jr. owned an early Buick, as did Bonnie Nowlin, J.C. Inzer, and Captain W.P. Lay. Otto Agricola could be seen driving an early Cadillac, and O.R. Hood enjoyed driving a Pierce Arrow. These were just some of the automobiles registered in Gadsden during the early days of the twentieth century.

These automobiles marked the beginning as well as the end of an era in the history of Gadsden. With the introduction of the automobile, the days of the riverboat trade were coming to a close. Transportation of goods and passengers soon shifted to the automobile. Improved roads and highways were just over the horizon, and the construction of traffic bridges soon also brought an end to the ferries across the Coosa River. The "Tin Lizzie," at first thought to be a passing fad, had propelled Gadsden into the new century.

In the early days of the 1900s, the public school system in Gadsden took a giant step toward improved education. In 1902, the Gadsden Board of Education voted to construct a new brick high school building in downtown Gadsden on the recommendation of board member Colonel R.B. Kyle. The school, named Disque High School in honor of Judge Disque, was located at the present site of the post office on Chestnut Street and was built at a cost of $11,952. The school originally had four large classrooms and an auditorium that seated 600 people.

Disque High School was erected on Chestnut Street in 1902. This beautiful brick structure, built at a cost of $11,952, was named in honor of Judge John H. Disque.

The first graduation exercise was held on May 26, 1902. The commencement address was given by Judge James Bilbro, father of Mathilde Bilbro, who later became a famous musician and composer. There were six graduates in this first class.

Judge John H. Disque was active during the early days of the twentieth century and served Gadsden in many capacities, including mayor more than once. Of the many titles Disque held in his lifetime, being president of the Gadsden Board of Education was his favorite. During the remaining years of his life, he constantly searched for ways to improve the public school system in Gadsden. Disque married Augusta G. Standifer, a daughter of Judge and Mrs. Lemuel Standifer, and his family lived in a beautiful home on the northwest corner of Fourth and Chestnut Streets in downtown Gadsden.

The year 1904 brought great improvements to the City of Gadsden, when one of the major problems with city government was addressed in April. By this time, a seat for city government had become a great necessity. The answer finally materialized in the building of the first Gadsden City Hall on North Fifth Street. The decision to build this structure was made during the administration of Mayor Robert Campbell. The aldermen were J.P. Armstrong, M.W. Moore, Lawrence Smith, C.L. Guice, and J.D. Dunlap.

During this time, the mayor and aldermen were also considering a petition submitted by irate citizens asking that all businesses be prohibited from opening on Sunday, and Mayor Campbell was asking for an extension of the city sewer system "in the interest of public health."

The Gadsden City Hall was completed late the following year during the administration of Mayor Charles P. Smith. The stately structure on North Fifth Street consolidated the

Gadsden's first city hall brought all of Gadsden's municipal offices under one roof. This building served as the seat of city government until the early 1960s.

city's municipal offices into one central location. The fire department and the police department were now located at city hall. The mayor's office was also relocated to the new municipal building. A beautiful dome crowned this magnificent structure, which served as the center of Gadsden's city government for the next 56 years.

The city hall also had a large courtroom where city court was held. Seats for this courtroom were purchased from Kyle's Opera House, which had suffered a destructive fire in 1902. The mayor's court heard a variety of cases, and many unusual fines were handed down here. The fine for allowing livestock to run at large in downtown Gadsden was $5. This was also the fine for the reckless driving of a horse and buggy. The fine for stealing chickens was $5 plus $2 in court costs. One person was brought into court for spitting on the sidewalk, but he was allowed to go free after a brief hearing. The fine for swinging on a moving train was $5, while the fine for visiting a house of ill repute was $1. Playing ball in the street was also a problem and carried a $2 fine. If a guilty party was unable to pay his fine, he was sentenced to work on the city streets and paid his fine off at the rate of 50¢ per day.

One of the major news stories of 1904 was the opening of the giant steel plant, a major employer in Gadsden for the next 96 years. This story actually had its beginnings back in 1902. The idea of locating a steel mill in Gadsden was the dream of Captain W.P. Lay, and it was through his efforts that the Southern Steel Company of Ensley relocated to this area. Lay had learned of the great deposits of iron ore and came up with the idea that this area would be a good place for a steel-making plant. Acting on this idea, he took the Schulers, George and E.T., into his confidence. These brothers were the active

In 1904, the Southern Steel Company, owned by George and E.T. Schuler, established a steel mill in the Gadsden area. The mill was the result of Captain W.P. Lay's efforts.

heads of the Southern Steel Company. Lay visited the Schulers in Birmingham to discuss relocating their steel plant to Gadsden.

At the suggestion of Lay, an expert on mines and steel production was sent to Etowah County to examine the prospects of locating a plant in the area. The expert was accompanied by Lay, who drove him throughout the county. A large vein of coal and iron was inspected and measurements were taken. The expert was so impressed with the resources that a recommendation was made to plant officials to locate a steel mill in Gadsden.

The Schulers visited the area and were impressed with the idea. They told Lay that if concessions could be secured, they would consent to move the plant. These concessions included the ability of the company to purchase the land of the Alabama Land and Development Company. Financial aid was sought to secure the properties, and through the efforts of Lay, Captain James M. Elliott Jr., Colonel A.T. Stocks, Colonel O.R. Hood, and other citizens, the funds were raised to secure the plant.

After the decision was reached to move the steel works to Gadsden, a problem arose in finding a suitable site. The first site considered was the old wagon works, although this area was much too small. East Gadsden was then visited, but this area was also ruled out because it could not be reached without crossing the river. Other areas were considered but ruled out for various reasons. It appeared that the plant would be lost before it could become a reality.

While the search was being carried out, the time arrived for the announcement of the plant. Lay invited a large group to the Bellevue Hotel on Lookout Mountain for dinner and made the announcement that a site had been found. Lay told of the water supply and the easy accessibility to the railroads. He also told of space for buildings and the possibility of digging a canal from the Coosa River to the plant site. After dinner, the group visited the proposed site and it was found to be satisfactory in every way.

The steel mill cost the city of Gadsden a total of $38,000 to secure. A blast furnace and four 50-ton open-hearth furnaces, with an annual rated capacity of 120,000 tons of ingots, were erected and the first steel was made in 1904.

In 1906, before the Schulers could finish moving their rod and wire mill from Ensley, they encountered financial difficulties and their Alabama Steel and Wire Company was forced to undergo a reorganization. It became the Southern Steel Company, which ran until the Panic of 1907, when the plant shut down. After two years of idleness, the company was again reorganized as the Southern Iron and Steel Company. A bar mill was added on Black Creek, as were two open-hearth furnaces, bringing the number to six.

In 1906, better health care came to the Gadsden area. During the early years of the 1900s, there were no hospitals in the area, although a "pest house" was operated in Gadsden. A pest house was a place where a person with a chronic ailment could go for health care.

The first public hospital to open in Gadsden was known as the Gadsden Infirmary, or the Guice and Faucett Infirmary. This hospital was opened by Dr. C.L. Guice, Dr. J.L. Gunter, and Dr. George W. Faucett in the old Denson home on Forrest Avenue. This new hospital opened on April 1, 1906, with 20 well-equipped patient rooms arranged to

The first public hospital in Gadsden was the Guice and Faucett Infirmary located in the old Denson home on Forrest Avenue. This hospital opened on April 1, 1906 with 20 rooms.

The Ralls Sanitorium was built on Sixth Avenue and Twelfth Street by Dr. A.W. Ralls and Dr. H.L. Ison at a cost of $6,000. Years later, this hospital would become the Baptist Hospital.

provide all the comforts that might be desired. More than $10,000 was spent turning the house into an infirmary.

In September 1906, a second hospital opened in the Gadsden area. Dr. A.W. Ralls built, at a cost of $6,000, a hospital on Sixth Avenue at Twelfth Street that he called the Ralls Sanitorium. This hospital was modern throughout and well equipped with every comfort suggested by science. The building had 29 rooms with steam heat, electric lights, water, and elevators. Dr. H.L. Ison was associated with Dr. Ralls in this venture.

These two hospitals both suffered destructive fires during the early years of existence. Dr. Ralls rebuilt and enlarged his hospital following this fire. Although these early hospitals were small and primitive, they paved the way for the modern hospitals of today.

Gadsden's first library began as a project by several young ladies known as the "Bachelor Girls." This group later became known as the Thursday Study Club. The group set out to open a public reading room and soon had purchased a small collection of books. This public reading room soon grew into Gadsden's first public library. The first reading room was located in the new Moragne Building located in the 400 block of Broad Street.

In 1904, an agreement was reached with the Carnegie Foundation for a $10,000 grant to build a public library in Gadsden. This was made possible through the efforts of Walter E. Striplin, superintendent of public schools. Striplin publicly solicited funds to purchase property on the northwest corner of Seventh Street and Forrest Avenue

Gadsden's first library was constructed in 1906 due largely to a $10,000 grant from the Carnegie Foundation. The library was dedicated on December 20, 1906. Lena Martin became the first librarian at the Gadsden Public Library.

for the library. After the property was purchased, the Carnegie Foundation donated the funds for this beautiful library, which was formally dedicated on December 20, 1906. Lena Martin became the first librarian at the Gadsden Public Library.

In December 1906, the first electric theater, or movie theater, came to the city. The first theater in Gadsden to advertise moving or motion pictures was the Electorium, which was located at 315 Broad Street and opened in early 1906. It was followed by two other theaters later that same month. The Nickelodium and the Theato, both located on Broad Street, opened in late December.

Several other movie houses opened in Gadsden in 1908. The Alamo Theatre at 506 Broad Street was very popular and was in operation for several years. The Pastime at 435 Broad Street was another early theater. The first large theater built in Gadsden was the Hayden-Pake Theatre. This theater, later known as the Gadsden Theatre, was located at 120 South Third Street and could seat 1,200 movie patrons.

In 1910, probably the most unusual theater opened in Gadsden. The Air-Dome Theatre, located on South Third Street next to the Hayden-Pake Theatre, was a canvas structure similar to a large circus tent. It seated 1,000 in comfort and offered both live shows and motion pictures. Another early theater, known as the Theato, was located at Canterberry Station in Alabama City.

The year 1907 saw many changes come to Gadsden. A beautiful monument was erected to honor the heroic act of Emma Sansom. This statue of Italian marble was created in Italy

The Emma Sansom Monument was erected in 1907. This marble statue was created at a cost of $3,750 and was dedicated on July 5, 1907.

at a cost of $3,750. A large crowd was on hand when the statue was dedicated on July 5, 1907. The monument was erected on a lot that was donated by the City, and the statue was placed so that Emma Sansom pointed toward Black Creek.

The dedication of the statue began at 10:00 a.m. with Mayor Dunlap making an address of welcome on behalf of the city. The unveiling was done by Mrs. A.V. Lee Sr., president of the local United Daughters of the Confederacy, and Mrs. Jennie Cain, a relative of Emma Sansom.

Public education was also making great strides during the year 1907. A new brick elementary school with a capacity of 400 students was built by the Gadsden Board of Education at a cost of $16,055. A public ceremony marked the placing of the cornerstone on May 9, 1907. The school was completed by September 1907, at which time, 282 pupils were enrolled.

The year 1907 was also a critical time in the life of downtown Gadsden. At this time, Gadsden was the site of several open saloons and was also the home of a distillery. Motlow's Saloon, operated by Spoon Motlow, was located in the 400 block of Broad Street and the Gadsden Distillery was located near Double Springs on Tuscaloosa Avenue. A temperance movement began in September 1907 in an attempt to close the saloons in Gadsden. A committee of some of Gadsden's most prominent citizens began circulating petitions and gathering names for a wet-dry vote. Names of more than 2,000 registered voters were turned in to Probate Judge J.W. Penn, who set a vote on the issue for October 29, 1907. On the day of this important vote, a large group of women and children turned

Motlow's Saloon was a popular local establishment before the temperance movement brought the days of the open saloon in Gadsden to a close.

Bill Echols's Saloon, located in the 400 block of Broad Street, was closed on December 31, 1907, by Sam O'Bannon.

out to lead the campaign for a dry vote. The vote stood 1,617 to 475 to close the saloons, and Gadsden became dry.

Gadsden's Mayor Robert Dunlap and Police Chief Sam O'Bannon pledged that the law in Gadsden would be strictly enforced. On December 31, 1907, the saloons were crowded, although no problems were encountered. Customers at Motlow's Saloon gathered to drink whiskey from an open barrel. At 10:00 p.m., Sam O'Bannon and the police moved to close down the saloons in Gadsden. Spoon Motlow moved to Chattanooga and advertised to send his Coosa River Whiskey back to his former customers. Lem Motlow moved to Lynchburg, Tennessee, to take a job with his uncle, Jack Daniels. Motlow became a master distiller at Jack Daniels.

During 1909–1910, one of the city's most beautiful structures was designed and erected on Broad Street. Gadsden's beautiful new post office was built on the southwest corner of Sixth and Broad Streets. It was originally planned to be a single-story structure built of reinforced masonry with a marble facing over a granite basement. The post office had a one-story entrance portico supported by paired columns. Work actually got underway in April 1909, with the building being completed in October 1910. A second and third floor were later added.

A major problem still facing the city was the condition of the streets. In 1907, concrete sidewalks were poured in downtown Gadsden to replace the stepping stones and wooden

Gadsden's new post office was built in 1909–1910. The structure was originally a one-story building, but a second and third floor were added later.

sidewalks, or "boardwalks." Curious townspeople were amazed at the new sidewalks and persisted in walking on them before the concrete set.

The problem of the city streets was finally addressed in 1909. A bill was passed to assess the cost of paving to the owners of the property along the streets. A store owner paid for the paving along his/her property, while the owner of the streetcar line paid for the paving along each side of the rails. This allowed each property owner to share in the cost of the work.

A foundation of chert and brick was used to pave Broad Street from Sixth Street to First Street. The paving began in late 1909 and continued with the paving of Chestnut Street and Forrest Avenue, which went until 1914. This paving project was a necessity because of the increasing numbers of automobiles in Gadsden. By 1915, there were 245 pleasure automobiles in the area and 48 commercial vehicles.

By the end of 1910, downtown Gadsden was taking on the look of a large town. Paving on the main street was beginning to slowly eliminate the major problems with the streets. A beautiful city hall had also combined all of the offices of municipal government into one building. The crown jewel of the early 1900s was the building of the new United States Post Office, located at 600 Broad Street.

Two other improved services that were offered during the early teens were in the form of a new county jail, built in 1910, and the purchase of new motorized fire engines, which were added to the Gadsden Fire Department in 1911.

The early Etowah County Jail was a brick building located on Chestnut Street and constructed in 1894. During the days of this early county jail, the sheriff lived at the jail in rooms allotted him by the county. By 1909, it was apparent that a new, larger jail was needed. The county commission met and voted to construct a new facility, and the new jail was built at 240 North Third Street, near the Etowah County Courthouse. Prisoners were transported back and forth between the jail and courthouse for their hearings and trials. If a person was sentenced to serve jail time, the sentence was carried out at the county jail. This early jail and also the "chain gang," with its hard labor, helped to deter crime and made it safe to walk the streets in downtown Gadsden.

Another service offered in Gadsden in 1911 was enhanced fire protection. In 1911, the city council voted to purchase the first motorized fire engine for the city. The money to purchase this fire engine was raised throughout the city by young girls who competed to raise the most money. The person who won the competition would have the engine named for her, with her name painted on the hood. Zera Lyles Appleton, the daughter of a prominent physician, won the contest and had the truck named "Zera Lyles" in her honor. In later years, the truck was repainted and a public outcry to replace the name forced the City to repaint it on the truck.

This fire engine was a four-cylinder, 1911 American LaFrance truck and was a welcome addition to the small fire department. The City also purchased another American LaFrance

The Etowah County Jail was located at 240 North Third Street and was the home of the county sheriff for a time. Prisoners frequently worked the streets of Gadsden as members of a chain gang.

The "Zera Lyles," Gadsden's first motorized fire truck, appears in the center. This was a 1911 American LaFrance fire engine.

pumper in 1914. During this time, when the City was attempting to upgrade and update the department, several fires proved the need for enhanced fire protection.

The year 1912 was an exciting time in Gadsden. The beautiful Bellevue Hotel had been purchased by Louis Hart, and plans had been put into place to open the grand hotel under the name of the Mineral Springs Hotel in June 1912. The hotel was preparing for the summer season when a tragic event took place on July 5, 1912. About 1:00 a.m., the night watchmen, making their rounds at the car works, noticed something unusual at the hotel on the brow of the mountain. Flames were discovered in the northwest wing of the huge hotel, and they spread quickly throughout the structure. Immediately, the watchmen began sounding the whistle at the car works as a warning and placed a call for help to the central fire station at city hall. The firetrucks were dispatched but turned back when they reached the foot of the mountain. At that time, there was no fire protection on the mountain and there was not a nearby source of water for the firetrucks to draft.

The fire was a spectacular sight, with flames leaping several hundred feet into the night sky. The blaze could be seen for many miles in every direction. The fire was so intense that nothing could be done except to watch the beautiful structure burn itself out. The cause of the fire at the Mineral Springs Hotel was never really determined. One probable cause was listed as electrical, although the Gadsden area had experienced a severe thunderstorm the previous day and much speculation was given to a possible lightning strike. The hotel was never rebuilt.

The ruins of the Mineral Springs Hotel are shown above. The hotel, built originally as the Bellevue Hotel, burned on July 5, 1912 at about 1:00 a.m. It was never rebuilt.

One special arrival in late 1912 would do much to help record Gadsden's early history. It was during this time that Adolph Lebourg and his wife, Annie Mae Lebourg, moved to the Gadsden area. Lebourg was a French immigrant who had come to the United States in 1908 when he jumped ship near New York.

Adolph Lebourg joined a circus and traveled south, bicycling to Alabama. During his travels, he learned English and basic photography. In 1909, he opened a photography studio in Piper, Alabama, where he offered photographic services to people living in the mining communities of Marvel, Coleanor, Belle Ellen, Savage Creek, Garnsey, and others.

Upon moving to Gadsden, Lebourg worked in the Krolinger Photography Studio until he was able to open his own studio in 1914. Lebourg was fascinated by photography and his work reflected his outstanding ability. Because of his love of photography, much of the history of downtown Gadsden was preserved. Lebourg took hundreds of photos of people, buildings, parades, trains, and motorcycles in Gadsden and the surrounding area.

Lebourg also owned and operated a bicycle shop on Broad Street. This store sold the finest bicycles and sporting goods in Gadsden. A big day in the life of downtown Gadsden was when the new "Indian" motorcycles came to town. A group of young men from Gadsden known as the "Gadsden Bunch" were seen riding their Indians everywhere.

Lebourg continued to be fascinated with photography and later purchased a movie camera. Many of the major events in downtown Gadsden were captured by Lebourg

Local photographer Adolph Lebourg recorded much of Gadsden's early history through the lens of his camera. Lebourg also loved his Indian motorcycle. (Courtesy of the Lebourg family.)

The "Whole Gadsden Bunch" could be seen riding their Indians all over town. This group participated in many endurance races. (Courtesy of the Lebourg family.)

on film, including the earliest glimpses of the steel plant as well as parades and even a Confederate veterans' reunion.

It was during this time that another Gadsden resident was doing his part to write his name in the local history books. J. Roy Hunt was the owner and operator of a small movie theater that opened at 505 Broad Street. This theater had opened during 1911, although it wasn't until 1915 that the popularity of this movie house took off. That was when Hunt purchased a movie camera and began filming things throughout North Alabama to show in his theater. Hunt also filmed a full-length movie feature starring local actors and actresses to show at the Belle Theatre. Hunt traveled extensively, shooting newsreels and perfecting his talents in cinematography. This made the Belle Theatre a very popular place, although success came at a high price because Hunt soon sold the Belle Theatre to Mr. and Mrs. W.B. Wood. Hunt later left Gadsden for Hollywood and a bright career as a cinematographer. Hunt actually filmed more that 150 movies, including the original version of *The Mighty Joe Young* and *I Walk with a Zombie.*

During October 1916, a young man from Alabama City was in negotiations with the Gadsden, Bellevue & Lookout Mountain Railroad Company to attempt a dive from the brow of Noccalula Falls to the pool below. Lowell Vickery was a high-diver who had already exhibited an unusual ability at making death-defying leaps into water. Vickery had inspected the falls and the water below and stated that this stunt could be completed without great risk or bodily harm. The distance from the brow of the falls to the pool below was a jump of 90 feet. The pool of water at the base of the falls was 20 feet deep. This stunt was held on July 4. Vickery, at this time, was only 19 years of age.

The Belle Theatre was a popular Broad Street theatre. It was owned, in its early days, by J. Roy Hunt and, later, by W. B. "Pop" Wood.

Daredevil Lowell Vickery jumped into a large tank of water from the clocktower of the Etowah County Courthouse. He also made many jumps from the crest of Noccalula Falls.

Vickery exhibited his unusual talents on more than one occasion. Along with Howard Shaneyfelt, Vickery made several jumps from the crest of the falls on Saturday and Sunday afternoons. Usually, Vickery would announce his intentions to jump in a loud voice while Shaneyfelt would pass the hat around to try to raise money "to bury the young daredevil in case something went wrong."

Vickery exhibited his uncanny ability on other occasions also. In a highly publicized stunt, he made a dive into a large tank of water from the clock tower at the Etowah County Courthouse on Broad Street. This stunt was done in front of a large crowd of curious onlookers. Although Vickery had made several jumps from greater heights, this leap left him badly bruised and shaken because the tank of water was not filled properly.

On still another occasion, Vickery announced that he would jump from the Louisville & Nashville Railroad bridge across the Coosa River. This jump was never allowed to take place, however, because local authorities intervened.

The city of Gadsden was the site of a large Confederate veterans' reunion on October 11, 1916. This was the first such reunion of its kind in Gadsden, and hundreds of veterans attended. Plans for this grand reunion had been finalized the year before when a delegation from Gadsden had attended the meeting in Selma to offer the city of Gadsden as host for the 1916 assembly.

The opening assembly was held at the Gadsden Theatre, and the auditorium was filled from the orchestra pit to the gallery. Following this meeting, a large parade was held downtown. Later that night, a dance was held on Broad Street in honor of the veterans, and the street was closed from Sixth Street to Seventh Street for the gala event.

In the the 1920s, Gadsden grew once again and took on even more of the characteristics of a larger city. An airfield in East Gadsden opened a new era of transportation to Gadsden in the form of the new fad known as the airplane. A former Gadsden resident who had become a pilot during World War I became one of the world's first stunt pilots. Milton Elliott lost his life in an airplane crash while filming a movie in California in 1920.

The Gadsden Board of Education was experiencing growing pains during the 1920s. By 1922, there was serious overcrowding at Disque High School. By the opening of the term in September, the overcrowding had grown to the point that 1,210 students attended school for only one-half day. Another 200 students were attending school in a church building, and another 160 students were attending school in two other rented buildings.

The problem was addressed by the school board with the sale of $250,000 in bonds to construct new schools. Contracts were awarded for the construction of the Etowah Avenue and South Gadsden schools, and planning was underway for the construction of a new high school for Gadsden.

On September 13, 1922, the board elected A.D. Simpson as the architect for the new high school. He had designed most of the school buildings in the city and had also been the resident architect on the construction of Dwight Manufacturing Company. On April 16, 1923, a contract was awarded to Baxter Brothers for the erection of the building, including the heating, plumbing, and wiring, for the sum of $148,500. The new school was completed on January 21, 1924, and opened to students on January 28, 1924. The

A large group of Confederates pose for a photo in front of the Emma Sansom Monument.

Gadsden High School, built to help eliminate the overcrowding at Disque High School, opened on January 28, 1924. A.D. Simpson was the building's architect.

The original home of the Holy Name of Jesus Hospital, this building on Chestnut Street housed the Gadsden General Hospital in earlier years.

new facility was formally opened to the public at a special program in February 1924. The new high school was named Gadsden High School and the old Disque High School was converted to a junior high school after serving 22 years as a high school.

On May 24, 1924, the first graduation exercises were held in the auditorium of the new school. For the first time in more than ten years, the high school could hold its graduation ceremony in a school auditorium. For several years, the Gadsden Theatre had to be rented to hold these exercises. Now the high school had the largest auditorium in the city.

A new hospital opened in Gadsden on January 2, 1925. This hospital started in a four-story, brick building on Chestnut Street that had actually been the home of the Gadsden General Hospital several years before. The facility was reopened by the Missionary Servants of the Most Blessed Trinity. The hospital was named for the day of its opening, which took place on the Feast of the Holy Name of Jesus. The Holy Name of Jesus Hospital had a rather humble beginning in Gadsden; records show that in the early days of this hospital, few patients were treated there.

The Gadsden area also suffered several destructive fires during the 1920s. The first of these was at the Gadsden Car Works, which burned in 1923. This was a blow to Gadsden's economy because the Gadsden Car Works, formerly the Elliott Car Works, was one of Gadsden's major industries. Two other destructive fires that affected the area during the

The aftermath of the destructive fire that closed the Gadsden Car Works in 1923 is seen above. This business's devastation was a major blow to Gadsden's economy.

The Printup Hotel suffered major fire damage in 1929. The Printup was renovated and reopened a short time later.

1920s hit the Printup Hotel. This grand hotel suffered fire damage in 1925 and major damage in February 1929. Each time, the Printup was renovated and continued to operate as one of Gadsden's major hotels. Alabama City also lost its only hotel when a destructive fire hit this beautiful wooden structure. The hotel burned during a steady, cold rain until it was reduced to smoldering embers.

Despite the major fires and tragedies of the 1920s, Gadsden was growing at a fast pace. In 1925, Gadsden's city limits were extended when East Gadsden was annexed on April 6. This caused a problem with the only bridge across the river being the railroad trestle. As early as 1923, the City of Gadsden was discussing a new traffic bridge across the Coosa River. A study was made in 1924 to explore the possibility of building a new bridge to eliminate the overcrowded traffic conditions on the railroad bridge.

In October 1924, Mayor W.E. Weir reported that the city's share in the cost of a new bridge would be $25,000. Work began on the new bridge in mid-1925. The bridge was constructed of reinforced concrete and was completed in early 1927. A four-day celebration took place on April 27 through April 30, 1927, to dedicate the beautiful Memorial Bridge.

One of the largest news stories of the 1920s came in late 1928. A committee consisting of O.R. Hood, A.P. Reich, Otto Agricola, W.P. Lay, Dr. A.W. Ralls, Louis Herzberg, and Louie Loveman had gone to Akron, Ohio, to secure a Goodyear plant for Gadsden.

Alabama Governor Bibb Graves speaks at the dedication of the Memorial Bridge across the Coosa River.

Because of the efforts of this delegation, Clifford Slusser and two other Goodyear officials, Charles Stillman and C.F. Stone, came to Gadsden to meet with local officials to make the announcement that Goodyear would build a plant in East Gadsden in 1929.

The ground-breaking ceremony at the plant site was held on January 1, 1929. Frank Steele of the Los Angeles, California Goodyear plant was named manager of the new Gadsden facility two days later. Actual construction of the plant began on February 7, 1929, and on June 21, 1929, four and one-half months following the ground breaking, the first tire rolled off the assembly line at the Gadsden plant. The formal dedication of the new Goodyear plant in Gadsden was held on July 11, 1929, and more than 10,000 people gathered on the premises for the event.

With the addition of this major industry, the future looked bright for the Gadsden economy. New jobs and new houses could be found in East Gadsden, which was made even more attractive by the beautiful new bridge spanning the Coosa River.

Colonel R.B. Kyle was quite active in many of the major business concerns in the Gadsden area throughout the late 1800s and into the early 1900s. Colonel Kyle amassed a huge fortune following the Civil War in the lumber business—his sawmills near the Coosa River cut between 80,000 and 100,000 feet of timber daily. Colonel Kyle also had large investments in local real estate, and at one time during the early part of the twentieth century, he owned over 200 dwellings of all classes in the Gadsden and Alabama City

The formal dedication for the Goodyear Tire and Rubber Company was held in Gadsden on July 11, 1929.

area. Kyle believed that one could not build a town without houses. He was instrumental in the establishment of the Gadsden Land and Improvement Company and the Gadsden Furnace Company, and he made sizable investments in the Printup Hotel and the Gadsden Paint Mill. In 1920, Colonel Kyle also founded the Kyle Real Estate Company, which would prove to be his final business venture.

Kyle remained active in local politics much of his life. Aside from serving three terms as mayor, he also served on the Gadsden School Board, was an alderman on one occasion, and represented the city as a delegate to the Alabama State Constitutional Convention of 1901. He was always ready to promote his home city to whomever he encountered on his many travels.

Colonel Kyle retired to his home on Lookout Mountain, although he never fully retired from public life. The final years of the colonel's life were spent at Whitehurst, his home overlooking the city. He was one of Gadsden's oldest and most beloved citizens when he passed away on January 7, 1922, at the age of 95, from pneumonia. The entire city closed its doors to attend his funeral at the First Baptist Church, where the colonel was a member. Reverend W.R. Rigell conducted the service, and Colonel Kyle was laid to rest in Forrest Cemetery.

Things came to an abrupt halt on November 29, 1929, the date of the great stock market crash that brought the national economy to a standstill. While the effects of this crash and panic were distant at first, they would soon come to be felt in Gadsden. This was a time when life savings were lost and banks and businesses failed. What had started as an era of growth and prosperity with the turn of the century turned into a troubling time, with a depression on the horizon by the close of 1929.

7. Depression and War

The decades of the 1930s and 1940s were remembered by many as some of the hardest times in the twentieth century. Gadsden experienced an era of growth as well as a time when many were out of work and homeless. During the Great Depression, businesses were forced to close, and a lot of people found themselves without a means of support. Without an income, people were forced to seek shelter from the cold and rain in any type of makeshift house that could be assembled with materials that were available.

"Hoover Towns" sprang up throughout the United States to house many homeless people. A "Hoover Town" was a small community of shanties that were constructed of cardboard, packing crates, or any other type of building material that was easily available. These shanty towns were named for President Herbert Hoover, on whom many placed the blame for the depression. One such community sprang up on the banks of Black Creek in Gadsden. Residents of Hoover Town were forced to hunt for food any way they could find it.

Although the early days of the depression were dark for Gadsden and Etowah County, soon the economy began to make a slow turnaround and several new businesses began to emerge. These businesses, along with the government programs, helped to keep Gadsden growing and working through this tough time.

By the early 1930s, the local economy was beginning to feel the bite of the depression, but it was not apparent to many because of the construction of a large skyscraper on the southwest corner of Broad and Seventh Streets. This building had been under construction since early 1929, with a completion date expected in August. The building, which housed Gadsden's Reich Hotel, was actually completed in February 1930 and was the largest building in Gadsden for many years. Adolph P. Reich, a resident of Gadsden who had spent much of his life in the hotel business, had planned to build this 10-story, 150-room hotel for several years. At the time of its construction, this beautiful hotel, made of brick and the most up-to-date materials, was one of the most modern hotels in the Southeast. Adolph Reich had earlier managed the Printup Hotel, which had been the largest hotel in Gadsden prior to the construction of the Hotel Reich.

The hotel was operated by Reich and a group of 250 investors. An interesting side note to the construction of this hotel was that many of the bricks used in the foundation of the hotel were taken from the old First Baptist Church building, which was located across

Hoover Town was located on the banks of Black Creek in Gadsden. These houses were made of cardboard and scrap lumber.

the street before it was torn down. The hotel also had a large parking garage, located at the rear of the building, that could accommodate 100 automobiles. A Gadsden girl, Vera Springfield, went to work at the Hotel Reich when it opened and worked there throughout the building's operation as a hotel.

As the local economy was beginning to slow down in the early 1930s, movie theaters were becoming the center of entertainment in Gadsden. Vaudeville shows were still popular at the Princess Theatre on Broad Street, and "Boob" Brasfield was a regular favorite on the stage at the still-popular Gadsden Theatre.

"Talking" movies had now totally replaced the silent movies of the 1920s. The Great Depression was beginning to take its toll on the local economy, and many businesses as well as the area theaters felt the impact of the hard times. To ensure the survival of the area movie houses, several master showmen were hired to manage the different theaters.

Gadsden's Princess Theatre had hired such a showman in the form of Dennis B. Dixon to help the theater remain open during the hard times. The Princess offered all types of outstanding attractions, from live shows and beauty contests to the finest in movie attractions. Bank Night was a local favorite, with cash being given away to a lucky movie patron. The Princess actually operated at a profit during these days, and the theater was renovated in 1937. The auditorium was enlarged and refurbished, and an Art-Deco facade was added to the exterior. The theater also added air conditioning. The Princess

Vera Springfield and manager M.M. Coates are pictured here assisting a guest in registering at the Hotel Reich.

The Hotel Reich was Gadsden's first skyscraper and opened in February 1930.

The popular Princess Theatre, pictured above during the early days of the 1930s, offered a variety of entertainment, from live vaudeville shows to the new motion pictures.

was now in the position to compete with the Gadsden Theatre as the best movie showplace in town.

Other theaters that were popular in Gadsden and Alabama City included the Capitol Theatre in downtown Gadsden and the Ritz Theatre and the Lyric Theatre in Alabama City. Most of the early movie theaters in Gadsden did not have concession stands or snack bars. Instead, small sandwich stands were usually located near the theaters where people could buy peanuts, popcorn, hot dogs, cigarettes, and candy to take inside the theater.

One such place of business was at 505 Broad Street, next to the Princess Theatre. This small business, owned by Julius M. Hansard, became famous for its hot dogs and was a downtown landmark for many years. Hansards became a favorite place for moviegoers in the downtown area, but it also offered a quick lunch for people working downtown. Hansards sold everything from soft drinks to tobacco but was famous throughout the area for its great hot dogs.

In later years, the theaters began to see the advantages in operating a concession stand inside the lobby of their theater. This caused businesses such as Hansards, which relied heavily on the movie patron, to relocate. Hansards moved across Broad Street next to the Capitol Theatre. Although the business had relocated, the great hot dogs were still the best in Etowah County.

Another interesting chapter in Gadsden's history was also written during the 1930s. It was during this period that a most unusual aircraft was making regular trips to the Gadsden

Hansards, located next to the Princess Theatre, sold the best hot dogs in town, along with other food and snack items.

area. With the coming of the Goodyear Tire and Rubber Company, the Goodyear blimp was soon to follow. A giant hangar was built on the Goodyear property behind the plant in East Gadsden to house one of the giant airships when it was in the area or during windy or stormy weather.

An air of excitement filled the entire city when the 192-foot-long airship visited the Goodyear plant. The roar of the huge engines usually announced its arrival before it could be seen. Children of all ages seemed to be fascinated by the blimp, and people came out by the hundreds to see it land and take off. Although the blimp was fun to watch, a small amount of risk was taken in landing the giant airship. On December 4, 1930, this became all too real for one Goodyear employee at the Gadsden plant.

The *Defender*, one of the ships in the air fleet, was due to arrive in Gadsden from Nashville, Tennessee, in the late afternoon. The blimp was usually weighted down with sand bags, although several had to be dropped off as the blimp fought a strong headwind between Nashville and Gadsden. The ship was unusually light because a total of 3,000 pounds of gasoline had to be used in the flight also. This made the airship extremely difficult to control.

Six men from the Gadsden plant were detailed to help land the giant blimp. In order to land, the craft would fly nose-down and close to the ground, and several men would grab ropes at the nose and tail of the ship to bring it to the ground. On this particular landing at the Gadsden plant, an unusual event took place. With the blimp nose down and close

The Goodyear blimp is shown in its hangar at the Gadsden Goodyear plant.

to the ground, the landing crew grabbed the lines to bring the airship in. A strong gust of wind caused the blimp to lunge upward. Two members of the landing crew did not turn loose of the landing lines, although the others shouted for them to do so. One of these helpless members of the landing crew did turn loose and fell about 25 feet to the ground suffering a broken back. The other member refused to turn loose and was carried up with the blimp.

The pilot of the *Defender* attempted to turn the blimp toward the Coosa River to drop the helpless man into the water. Iken Douglas Phillips, a 27-year-old Goodyear employee, held on to the rope for about 10 minutes before falling about 150 feet to his death. After the accident, the *Defender* was brought down and guided to its hangar without further difficulty.

Another interesting story dealing with aircraft took place during 1931, when Gadsden acquired its first real airport. An airfield was constructed on property owned by Republic Steel in South Gadsden near the rear of the steel plant. This airport had a large wooden hangar and a runway where small- to medium-sized airplanes could land and take off.

This landing field was used throughout the 1930s as Gadsden's airport, and people often came out to the airfield to watch the planes land and take off. Interest was always high, and young and old alike were fascinated by the airplanes. The city of Gadsden had taken its first real steps into modern times with the building of this first landing field and small airport.

Gadsden had grown quite a bit since its first taste of the airplane craze following the days of World War I. The first airfield in the area was a large ball field in East Gadsden, and now Republic Steel had built a more modern airfield for the people of Gadsden. This early "airport" served Gadsden well for the next several years as the city progressed into the age of air travel.

Another exciting event that took place during 1931 was the dedication of the beautiful new Holy Name of Jesus Hospital. The Holy Name of Jesus Hospital was originally known as the Gadsden General Hospital, which was located in the 500 block of Chestnut Street in downtown Gadsden. This hospital was in operation for several years when it was purchased by Mary Wall of Pittsburgh for $50,000 and was deeded to the Missionary Servants of the Most Blessed Trinity. By 1930, the hospital was seeing hundreds of patients and the staff at this time numbered 20 doctors.

As Gadsden took on its new industrial life, the need arose for a larger hospital. Moragne Park was purchased for the site of the new hospital, and work began there on July 2, 1930. J.P. Burke of Springfield, Illinois, served as general contractor on the construction of this new building. Over the next several months, this beautiful hospital, overlooking the Coosa River, began to take shape.

The modern Holy Name of Jesus Hospital was formally dedicated on September 14, 1931. The tall, white building, with its 120-bed capacity, was brought to completion through the cooperation and assistance of the doctors, nurses, and citizens of Gadsden.

Republic Steel built an airfield that served as one of Gadsden's airports during the 1930s.

The new Holy Name of Jesus Hospital was dedicated on September 14, 1931.

The green cross was lighted to tower over the city as a symbol of love and merciful care to the sick and injured.

Over the years, the Holy Name of Jesus Hospital had developed and grown with the city of Gadsden. From its beginning as a 25-bed hospital in 1925 to its new 120-bed facility, the staff and management of this hospital attempted to meet the growing needs of a growing community.

By the early 1930s, the depression was beginning to take its toll on the city government in many small towns throughout the country. Many were finding it difficult to offer services such as police and fire protection as well as provide for basic educational needs. To complicate matters, many businesses began to close and local residents began to lose their jobs. The rise in unemployment slowly began to affect the budgets of local municipalities, and many services offered by the cities were interrupted. This was the case in the mill village of Alabama City. The school system in Alabama City had grown to meet the increasing needs of the growing town. Alabama City now had the Dwight Grammar School and the Elliott Grammar School, as well as the Emma Sansom High School, which was built in 1929. These schools caused such a hardship on the small town's budget that by 1932, when a consolidation attempt once again came up, the mayor and aldermen endorsed merging with Gadsden.

The Dwight Manufacturing Company had grown into one of the largest textile mills in the United States and employment was at an all-time high. The population of Alabama City had been steadily growing since the mill had first come to the town. Canterberry

Station and Wall Street were thriving with businesses of all types and things seemed to be running smoothly for the city government led by Alabama City Mayor Raymond Morgan. The ever-increasing cost of the Alabama City schools changed this as the depression continued to take its toll.

Over the years, several attempts had been made to consolidate the cities of Attalla, Alabama City, and Gadsden, although resistance to this merger was fierce. An attempt to combine the towns had emerged on at least two occasions with little interest being shown by local citizens. Alabama City and Attalla seemed content to keep their separate identities and the talk of merger was soon forgotten. In 1926, a committee was formed to look into merging Alabama City and Gadsden when a renewed interest was shown for the consolidation. Mayor R.A. Burns of Alabama City endorsed a resolution drafted by the Alabama City City Council opposing the idea. The attempt was made again in 1929. The proposal came to a vote and was defeated by the residents of Alabama City, 422-51.

With the effects of the depression lingering on and Alabama City unable to meet its payroll, the only solution appeared to be a merger with Gadsden. This was felt by many to be the most workable solution to the financial problems being faced by the Alabama City government.

Although many residents of Alabama City were still opposed to even the talk of a merger, another vote did come about on July 12, 1932. Mayor R.D. Morgan believed the merger with Gadsden would help to relieve the financial crunch being felt by the citizens of Alabama City. The vote once again showed a large margin, but this time the citizens of Alabama City voted 520-153 in favor of merging with Gadsden. Alabama City officially became part of the City of Gadsden on July 13, 1932.

Raymond D. Morgan was Alabama City's last mayor.

This merger brought about many benefits, including easing the financial pinch being felt by the Alabama City school system. The city of Gadsden now had a population of more than 32,000 residents. Several schools were also added to the Gadsden city system through the merger, including a practically new Emma Sansom High School. The total property value of Gadsden also increased in this merger by $2 million. Gordon Cantrell was elected associate commissioner for Alabama City for the remaining term of the Gadsden City Commission.

The dream of Captain James M. Elliott Jr. had been partially achieved when Alabama City and Gadsden merged in July 1932. This merger brought about financial stability for the school system of Alabama City and a growth in both property and population for the city of Gadsden. Because of the wisdom of the leaders of Alabama City and Gadsden, this great city continued to prosper during the dark days of the Great Depression.

A new industry came to Gadsden despite the economic hardships of the 1930s. Tro-Fe Dairy was founded in 1932 by Vern Troutman and Fred Feger. (The name Tro-Fe was a combination of the two founder's names.) The original location of the dairy was on Henry Street. This partnership did not last long, however, and Vern Troutman soon purchased Feger's interest and assumed sole ownership of the dairy. Troutman was a very bold businessman to enter into this commercial endeavor during the years of the depression. Troutman believed for his business to survive, he had to have a quality product, a reliable source, capable plant personnel, reliable salesmen, and a demand for his product.

Tro-Fe Dairy offered a wide variety of high-quality products. The dairy was the first in Gadsden to offer pasteurized milk. In the days prior to this, people drank raw milk.

Tro-Fe Dairy was founded by Vern Troutman and Fred Feger.

During the latter part of 1936, Tro-Fe Dairy requested a permit to build a new structure on Walnut Street. Although there was some local opposition to Tro-Fe Dairy locating there, the City did not stop the yellow-brick building from being constructed. The dairy offices were in a large house that was located next to the main building. Later additions made the dairy a distinctive landmark in downtown Gadsden.

Tro-Fe Dairy offered home delivery to a large area. During the late 1930s, home delivery was offered seven days a week because many people in the area did not yet have refrigerators. Ice boxes were still found in many homes throughout Etowah County. At its peak, the dairy had 38 delivery routes and more than 20,000 customers.

In the early days of home delivery, the trucks were small and bottles of milk were packed in shaved ice. In later years, these small delivery trucks were replaced by larger, refrigerated trucks. Home delivery had an advantage because sales tax did not have to be paid on the milk purchases. Everything was delivered in those days in glass bottles—whole milk, buttermilk, and chocolate milk. The milkman delivered the milk and picked up the empty bottles from the previous delivery. People were encouraged to return the empty bottles as clean as possible.

Tro-Fe Dairy did much for the local community. Maps were given out to all grammar school students for many years. Tours were also offered to school groups, and Tro-Fe Dairy sponsored many school functions during its existence.

January 23, 1934, was a date that would be remembered by many in Gadsden for years to come since it marked the end of an era in the history of Gadsden—the day the last streetcar operated in Gadsden. Streetcars had been operating in Gadsden for almost 48 years when the decision was made to discontinue this service because the streetcars, or trolleys, were no longer operating at a profit.

Colonel R.B. Kyle had petitioned the Gadsden City Council for a permit to operate a street railway in 1886, and the first mule-drawn streetcars went into service the following year. In 1888, work was underway to convert these slow-moving cars into a steam dummy line. Captain James Elliott purchased the railway in 1890 and converted it to electric power in 1899. The streetcar line was purchased by W.H. Weller and C.S. Ward in 1900 and remained under their ownership until the Alabama Power Company purchased it during the 1920s. Then, the decision was made to discontinue the streetcars, with the final run being made on the Cansler Avenue route. Other routes included the Walnut Street route and the Ewing Avenue–North Gadsden route.

The streetcars had become a part of life in Gadsden, Alabama City, and Attalla. For years, students in Alabama City depended on the streetcar to go to high school in either Gadsden or Attalla before the building of Emma Sansom High School. When high school football came to the area, the streetcars made special runs to bring people to Elliott Park from Gadsden and Attalla to see these first games. When special features were showing at the Gadsden Theatre or Princess Theatre, special late cars ran to provide transportation to Alabama City and Attalla so that people could go to the show. Many everyday happenings through the years were associated with the streetcars.

But on January 24, 1934, a new transportation era began in Etowah County. Beginning at 5:00 a.m., Crescent Motors began operating a bus line between Gadsden and Attalla. The buses operated along the same routes as had the streetcars. In fact, many of the former

The last streetcar run in Gadsden took place on January 23, 1934.

employees of the street railway were given jobs on the bus line. Crescent Motors was given a 25-year franchise by the Gadsden City Commission.

Federally funded programs also brought growth to the Gadsden area during the mid-1930s. The aim of these programs was to put people to work, thus easing the hardships of the depression. The programs helped keep unemployment down and also helped to stimulate the economy.

In Gadsden, these programs provided many new buildings. One such structure was Gadsden's Municipal Auditorium, which was constructed in mid-1935 overlooking the Coosa River. The Municipal Auditorium, or Convention Hall, is located next to the Gadsden Amphitheatre, which was also a product of government programs such as the Works Progress Administration (WPA) and the Public Works Agency (PWA). These agencies provided jobs in the form of labor, and this labor produced many memorable and attractive buildings throughout the United States.

The amphitheater was built in Gadsden in 1935 at an estimated cost of $10,000. The structure, made of native pink sandstone, was built in Legion Park and could seat 1,700 patrons. Its construction provided work for 40 men for a period of two months.

The Gadsden Amphitheatre was designed by Paul Hofferbert, a prominent local architect who designed many schools and public buildings in the Etowah County area. The amphitheater was designed to provide a suitable and conveniently located place for civic functions. The site that had been selected was a portion of the property on the banks of the Coosa River formerly owned by Etowah County Post No. 5, American Legion,

Gadsden's Municipal Auditorium was built in mid-1935.

The Gadsden Amphitheatre was a product of federally funded works projects.

adjacent to South First Street. The Legion Park Bowl, or Gadsden Amphitheatre, had stage facilities that could accommodate any ordinary play, pageant, or similar performance; dressing facilities were also provided.

The stage was constructed with a suitable roof and background for proper acoustic effects. Built of stone, the stage was also equipped with electrical fixtures of modern design, so that plays, motion pictures, and other performances could be seen at night. This beautiful facility was the site of concerts, plays, wrestling events, and high school graduations during the next several years.

The Chapel at Forrest Cemetery was also a product of the public works programs of the 1930s. Erected in 1935, the chapel was constructed of pink sandstone that was quarried on Lookout Mountain near Gadsden. The unique construction of the chapel also called for the shingles of the roof to be made of pink sandstone.

The Gadsden Board of Education was adding new schools during the depression years of the 1930s. A new and modern high school was built in West Gadsden near the foot of Lookout Mountain for the black students of Gadsden. This school was entered for the first time on September 23, 1936, and had a registration list of 1,017 pupils. Robert Hatch was the first principal at Carver High School, and McDonald Hughes was a coach and assistant principal.

A new Dwight Elementary School was also built in 1936. This school was a large, two-story brick building on Cabot Avenue and replaced the aging three-story structure that had been built by the Dwight Manufacturing Company. Other new schools built

The Chapel at Forrest Cemetery was made of pink sandstone with sandstone shingles.

Carver High School, which opened on September 23, 1936, was led by Robert Hatch, its first principal.

during the depression included the West Gadsden Elementary School and the Gulfsteel Junior High School. Gulfsteel Junior High School was erected near the site of the Emma Sansom homeplace in Alabama City.

During the 1930s, the Gadsden Board of Education struggled at times but continued to grow and add new schools to the city system. These new schools helped to provide enhanced education opportunities for the children growing up in Gadsden.

By January 1940, things were starting to look up throughout the United States. The economy was beginning to turn around and businesses on the local scene were once again growing and becoming profitable. The rest of the world and the rumblings of war across the ocean in Europe seemed light years away; in fact, the main concern in the United States was a severe cold spell.

On Monday, January 22, 1940, the daytime temperature hovered around freezing and the nighttime temperature dropped into the teens. The weather forecast for the night of the 22nd called for slightly warmer temperatures with a chance of sleet or snow possible. Residents in the Gadsden area went to sleep on Monday night with only a threat of winter weather. What they woke up to was the harsh reality of the destructive force of Old Man Winter. Most citizens remember the storm starting out as rain and sleet although it changed to snow about 11 o'clock.

The next morning, Gadsden woke to a blanket of white. To the delight of school-age children, at least 11 inches of fresh snow covered everything, with more expected

The frozen Coosa River is shown here following a heavy snow in 1940. Men are "walking" on the water.

throughout the day. This was the heaviest snow in more than a quarter of a century in Gadsden, and it brought everything to a complete standstill. The schools in Gadsden were closed by Superintendent C.A. Donehoo, who announced that classes would resume on Thursday.

The heavy snow and sub-freezing temperatures made travel on the streets and highways in the area extremely hazardous. City street crews used a makeshift snowplow to attempt to open the streets in downtown Gadsden. Many city employees were put to work shoveling the sidewalks in the downtown business district, although snow fell throughout the next day.

Commission President J.H. Meighan had a narrow escape from serious injury when his car swerved at the intersection of Sixth and Locust Streets and was almost struck by a passing freight train. Meighan was on his way to work at city hall early that morning. The Etowah County Courthouse and Gadsden City Hall were open, although no one ventured out into the weather.

The official measurement of the snow was listed at 12 inches, and this heavy snowfall virtually brought business to a grinding halt throughout the state. By Wednesday, January 24, the temperature began to drop again, dipping to near zero. Traffic on the streets remained at a standstill, and many travelers found themselves stranded at the bus terminal and train depot.

By Saturday, conditions had improved little, with the temperature dropping to near zero at night and rising to only the low 20s during the daylight hours. The Coosa River was frozen over for the first time since 1899. Ice covered the entire width of the river in North Gadsden near the waterworks plant. Water was frozen solid near the edges of the Memorial Bridge in downtown Gadsden. To make matters worse, coal supplies in the city were beginning to run dangerously low.

A ray of hope appeared on Sunday morning as a prediction of warmer temperatures and fair skies greeted the people of Gadsden. For a week the weather had dealt the Gadsden area a near death blow. Beginning Sunday, a slow warming trend gradually allowed North Alabama to dig out of its deep freeze.

By early 1940, it was beginning to be obvious to most people that the United States was not going to remain neutral in the war that was raging in Europe. With the ever-increasing threat of war, a major industry soon came to East Gadsden that would employ several hundred residents during the war years.

The Gadsden Ordnance Plant, or "shell plant" as it was known by most people who worked there, was among an early group of facilities that was authorized by Congress in 1940. General L.H. Campbell met with civic leaders during September of that year to look over a number of possible sites in the Etowah County area suitable for a government plant for the production of high-explosive artillery shells.

A large tract of land was selected for this plant in East Gadsden on the Gadsden-Anniston Highway. This parcel of land covered an area of 330 acres and was purchased by the Department of Defense; construction of the munitions plant was begun immediately. The plant, when completed and equipped, represented an

The Gadsden Ordnance Plant, or shell plant, opened on October 9, 1941.

initial investment of $7 million in the local economy. At that time, the Gadsden plant was the largest government-owned establishment devoted exclusively to the forging and making of shells.

There were 23 buildings in this industrial site. The area was enclosed with a high protective fence, well lighted, and heavily patrolled. Other protective features included the buildings being spread out over a large area and all utilities being run underground.

The two main manufacturing buildings were the forge shop and the machine shop. The forge shop was 150 feet by 500 feet and contained 11 forging lines. The machine shop was a large 300-by-500–foot building and was a typical "blackout" building, having no windows. This building was air conditioned and was lighted by more than 3 miles of fluorescent lighting. Other buildings on the compound included a fire station, a warehouse, a garage, a sewage disposal plant, and the main office building.

The Gadsden Ordnance plant was officially dedicated on October 9, 1941, less than two months before the United States entered World War II. Once in operation, the plant produced shells for the military's 105-mm cannon. When production first started, workers produced between 400 and 800 shells per shift. By the end of 1941, the total had increased to 1,400 shells per shift. The shell casings were manufactured at the Gadsden plant, and the powder for the shells came from Childersburg. The powder and shell casings were then sent to Lone Star, Texas, where the different components were assembled. More than 16 million shells were manufactured here during the war years.

Another indication that the United States was preparing for war came in formal announcement that the Etowah County area had been chosen for a new military installation. Little did anyone dream that the announcement of Etowah County's selection as the site for this new base would come just a few days before the United States would be plunged into war.

The announcement that a large chemical warfare training facility would be located in Etowah County was made on December 2, 1941. This announcement came just before the Japanese attacked the U.S. Pacific fleet and the naval base at Pearl Harbor on December 7, 1941. The site that the U.S. Army had chosen for the training facility was a 36,000-acre tract of land near Gadsden and Attalla. The camp was situated between U.S. 411 and U.S. 11 from Big Wills Creek in Attalla to near Ashville in St. Clair County.

The camp was named for General William Luther Sibert, a native of Etowah County and a graduate of the U.S. Military Academy. Sibert was instrumental in the construction of the Gatum Locks in the Panama Canal. The Chemical Warfare Training Center was dedicated on December 25, 1942, when the camp was 80 percent complete. This facility was built at a cost of $16.6 million. During the days of 1943, the camp contained 1,500 buildings and 41 miles of roads. Camp Sibert, at times, housed as few as 5,000 troops, but could accommodate as many as 30,000. It also housed a prisoner-of-war camp that held up to 500 POWs. In the later years of the war, ten members of Hitler's SS troops were held at the camp.

During World War II, several famous entertainers performed at Camp Sibert. Red Skelton and Mickey Rooney visited, and Joe Louis fought an exhibition for the troops stationed there. The camp contributed much to the local economy of Etowah County.

Above is one of the gates to Camp Sibert, which was dedicated on December 24, 1942.

Hundreds of civilian jobs were created, and the thousands of men stationed at the camp spent hundreds of dollars in Gadsden. In September 1943, Amelia Harris of the Women's Army Corps arrived to train the first five members of the WAC at Camp Sibert.

During the years of the war, both fighter planes and medium-range bombers were housed at Camp Sibert. A large airfield was located on the military installation.

When World War II came to a close, the need for so many military installations also ended. Camp Sibert was officially closed on December 31, 1945. The airfield at the base was turned over to the City of Gadsden and became the Gadsden Municipal Airport.

While Gadsden and the surrounding county was helping to prepare for international war with the opening of the Gadsden Ordnance Plant and Camp Sibert, many people were also doing their part at home in the early 1940s. Changes came rapidly for people living in Gadsden during these days. For the first time in years, many local citizens felt a real threat to the freedom that so many had taken for granted. This prompted local city governments, in conjunction with the federal government, to take precautions against a possible attack.

Gadsden was considered a possible target for attack because of the steel plant and Goodyear. These industries, along with the shell plant and several others, made the Etowah County area a prime target for attack or possibly a terrorist strike. To guard against this, an auxiliary civil defense police force was suggested to serve as air raid, or blackout, wardens. The job of this group was to aid in blacking out the city in the event of a possible air raid. The responsibility of forming and training such a force fell on the shoulders of Carl M. Cook, a Gadsden police officer.

Mayor J. Herbert Meighan was contacted by the military about forming the Civil Defense Auxiliary Police Force, and Meighan turned to Carl Cook, the police force's radio dispatcher since 1934 and a communications expert. He was given 30 days in which to enlist a force of up to 400 members. The job of this group was to assemble at a moment's notice and to "black out" as many of the lights of the city as quickly as possible.

To form such a unit, Cook enlisted L.L. Blackwood to serve as the chief of this auxiliary police force. Two captains were then enlisted and a total of 400 members were chosen. This group was then very well trained and actually won second place as one of the best in the United States.

On a given night, the call came into the Gadsden City Hall from Fort Sam Houston, Texas, for a blackout drill. Cook immediately called Blackwood of the auxiliary police force. Blackwood then called his captains who alerted the rest of the force. The group then took to the streets to black out the town. The drill was completed in less than 20 minutes.

This force was used throughout World War II. Its members gave much of their time to performing this worthwhile job and received only one barbecue dinner and the helmets that they wore as compensation for their time and energy. This group of unpaid volunteers served their city well during a difficult time.

When the harsh days of World War II arrived, the Gadsden area was well prepared though the next four years still caused hardships for many residents. And though many had hoped that the war would never involve the United States and any of her sons and daughters, the reality of World War II came to Gadsden on October 31, 1941.

One person who became involved in the horror of the war was Gadsden police officer Frank Towers, a native of Leesburg in Cherokee County. He enlisted in the U.S. Navy

Members of the Civil Defense Auxiliary Police, this group of "black out" wardens served unpaid during the days of World War II.

at an early age and served one stint before returning to this area. He took a position as a Boaz policeman, a job he performed until he accepted a similar position with the Gadsden Police Department. Towers moved to Gadsden and walked a beat in the downtown area until he was called back to active duty with the Navy in May 1941.

Towers was assigned to the USS *Reuben James* as a chief gunner mate. The *Reuben James* was a 21-year-old destroyer escort that was assigned to patrol an area just west of Iceland. At this time, German submarines were taking a heavy toll on British shipping in the North Atlantic. The *Reuben James* was escorting a convoy on October 31, 1941, when a German submarine slammed at least two torpedoes into the hull of the destroyer escort, sending it to the bottom of the sea in a matter of minutes. This was actually the third U.S. warship to be fired upon by the Germans and the second one to be hit. On October 17, 1941, the destroyer *Kearny* had survived a torpedo blow amidship, but the *Reuben James* was not as fortunate as the *Kearny*. The German torpedoes sank the *Reuben James* with a heavy loss of life. The ship carried a crew of 6 officers and 114 men.

The dreaded news came to Frank Towers's family in Gadsden that the young man had been killed in action. Frank Towers was remembered as a good police officer; he was well liked and well respected by members of the downtown business community, where he walked a beat on Broad Street. A bronze star was placed near the corner of Third and Broad Streets to honor the memory of the former Gadsden police officer who lost his life in the service of his country during the days just before the United States's entry into World War II.

Hundreds of people from Gadsden and Etowah County served their country well during World War II. Many paid the ultimate price for freedom and never returned home. With the end of the war in 1945, the Gadsden area once again experienced a time of growth and prosperity. Although the city was growing, the sacrifices that had been paid by so many were not soon forgotten.

8. Baby Boomers

The date was August 14, 1945, and the news was beginning to spread throughout the entire city of Gadsden that the Japanese had surrendered, bringing about an end to World War II and four years of fighting in Europe, North Africa, and the South Pacific for hundreds of Etowah County residents. This also meant the close of the Gadsden Ordnance Plant and Camp Sibert, which had brought many jobs and much revenue to Gadsden. The city reaped many benefits from Camp Sibert, including the air field that became the Gadsden Municipal Airport when the property was officially deeded to the City by the government.

Following the end of the war, many men and women from Gadsden came home to resume their lives in a peace-time America. In the months that followed, Gadsden residents returned to take up their jobs at the cotton mill, steel plant, and Goodyear. Times slowly began to return to normal, and Gadsden was preparing to enter another phase of growth. This time of development saw people finding new ways to enjoy their free time, such as drive-in theaters and professional baseball. The economy was strong and people once again began to enjoy the simple pleasures that everyday life had to offer. While the early 1940s were marked by military installations and munitions plants throughout the country, the latter part of the decade saw these closed and private businesses once again going strong.

Local ice cream parlors were very popular during the late 1940s and on into the 1950s. Two of these popular establishments were Crossfield's and Wrenn's Ice Cream. Owned and operated by Louis Crossfield, Crossfield's was located on Forrest Avenue in West Gadsden near downtown and was a very popular place for teens to meet. The ice cream that was made here was high quality and very popular throughout Etowah County.

Another popular place to go in Gadsden for great ice cream was Wrenn's Ice Cream Company, located at 1108 Forrest Avenue. Owned and operated by Robert E. Wrenn, Wrenn's made their own ice cream, which was famous throughout the Gadsden area for its great flavor. Ice cream at Wrenn's sold for 15¢ a pint and 25¢ a quart. Many people remember the tasty milkshakes that could be purchased there for 25¢. Most drive-in restaurants in the area offered malts and milk shakes made with Wrenn's famous ice cream. Crossfield's and Wrenn's are even remembered today for their superb locally made product.

Crossfield's Ice Cream Parlor, located at 1210 Forrest Avenue, was a popular place to go for great ice cream.

In 1946, the City of Gadsden finally obtained the property on Lookout Mountain that contained the area's top tourist attraction. It was at this time that 169 acres of land containing the beautiful Noccalula Falls was purchased from Sadie Elsmore. The property had been owned by the R.A. Mitchell family since 1909. Mitchell, a former Gadsden mayor, had recognized the value of this property and had hoped to see the City of Gadsden one day own this natural resource. Gadsden purchased the property for $70,000 and an additional 80 acres of land for $12,500 in October 1949. Because of the efforts of R.A. Mitchell, Noccalula Falls—with its natural beauty, Indian legends, and scenic grandeur—were opened to residents of Gadsden and the surrounding area for many years to come.

Also in 1946, Gadsden once again ventured into the world of professional baseball. Several attempts had been made to field a local team through the years, although these teams had met with little success. Gadsden's next entry would prove to be the most entertaining and successful by far. A group of local investors had been negotiating with the Memphis Chicks of the Southern League to bring a Class B baseball team to Gadsden to compete in the Southeastern League. The Chicks were to provide some of the players for this team, although the nucleus of the team could be signed from local talent. Byron Todd was named president, and he set out to put together a competitive team.

Barney Bridgers was a popular member of the Gadsden Pilots, a local Class B baseball club. (Courtesy of the Bridgers family.)

A contest was held to name the new team, with the winner receiving a season's pass to all home games. The name chosen for Gadsden's entry into the Southeastern League for the 1946 season was the Pilots. This name was chosen because of Gadsden's rich heritage associated with the riverboats and the Coosa River.

Dave Coble, the team's first manager, set out to find as much talent as possible by the opening day of spring training. The Pilots reported for spring drills in Henderson, Texas, on March 1, 1946. Many promotions were held to market the franchise in the days leading up to the season opener, and the front office was quite optimistic as the season opener drew near. The Gadsden Pilots were to open the season with a game in Anniston against the Anniston Rams.

A group of seasoned veterans took the field on March 19, 1946, to open the season with a three-game series against the Rams. The Pilots won the season opener, 5-3, and followed with a 5-4 win in game two. The Pilots celebrated this early victory by thrashing the Rams 11-1 in game three.

The Pilots were very competitive during their first season in the Southeastern League, and the team carried a .290 batting average during that time. Five members of the Pilots were among the top hitters in the league during their first season. Roy Pinkston led the Pilots with a .350 batting average and 33 home runs. George Brown led the league with 52 doubles while scoring 102 runs and batting .336.

The Pilots infield was anchored by shortstop Byron "Barney" Bridgers. Acquired from Fresno in the Pacific Coast League, Bridgers quickly became a local favorite. Bridgers was originally a signee of the St. Louis Cardinals. Another favorite was local Clarence Harkins, who split his playing time between third base and the outfield.

During the 1946 season, the Pilots raced out to an early lead only to have injuries to key players take a toll on the team down the stretch. In the first season, the Pilots finished in sixth place with a 60-76 record. Lee Blaine was the voice of the Pilots, broadcasting the games locally.

A new era was also beginning for the movie theaters in the Gadsden area. Downtown Gadsden still had the Gadsden Theatre, Capitol Theatre, and the beautiful Princess Theatre, along with the Gem Theatre, which had opened on North Sixth Street for black movie patrons. Competition was intense for the moviegoer's dollar, and the theaters featured all types of promotions to lure people into their places of business.

The Gadsden Theatre was the oldest theater in the city at this time. This movie house was still producing live shows starring Boob Brasfield and his daughter Bonnie. People by the hundreds were still coming in to see these shows. The Princess Theatre, managed by D.B. Dixon, was running a fierce competition with the Gadsden Theatre. The Princess was "the" place to go in downtown Gadsden for many years. The Capitol Theatre was a smaller theater that was famous for showing great Western movies.

The Hayden-Pake Theatre, later known as the Gadsden Theatre, was the first large theatre built in Gadsden. Located at 120 South Third Street, it could seat 1,200 movie patrons.

A large crowd of young people anxiously await the opening of the Princess Theatre, which was popular in Gadsden from the late 1920s until the early 1960s.

Something happened on September 26, 1947, that made the rivalry heat up between the movie theaters in Gadsden. On this date, a new movie house opened, and there was a drastic change for moviegoers in the area. Gadsden's new Pitman Theatre became the newest addition to downtown Gadsden. This movie house was owned and operated by C.S. Pitman from Pine Mountain, Georgia.

Pitman owned several theaters in Alabama and Georgia and was looking to open a new theater in the Gadsden area, which was thought to be a good market for a new theater. The location chosen for the Pitman Theatre was on the 600 block of Broad Street on property owned by local ophthalmologist H.W. Frank.

Built with concrete, marble, and brick, this beautiful movie house was made with the finest materials available. It was also praised for its construction of fire-resistant materials. Some of the luxuries that the Pitman offered were air conditioning, push-back seats, and the largest screen in Gadsden.

The 850-seat auditorium was packed on opening night for the movie feature *Slave Girl*, starring Yvonne DeCarlo and George Brent. A large group of dignitaries and special guests were on hand for the opening. With the opening of the Pitman Theatre, a friendly, but intense rivalry soon began between the management of the Princess and the Pitman. Initially, the Pitman had trouble getting first-run movies, while D.B. Dixon at the Princess got his choice of films. The first really big movie the Pitman landed was *The Babe Ruth*

Story on the theater's first anniversary. As the Pitman began to get better movies, Dixon could be seen standing out front of the Princess with binoculars trying to see how long the line was at the Pitman Theatre.

Through the years, moviegoers have benefited from the many great promotions that theater owners have dreamed up to make their theater the one to attend. On October 2, 1947, a new twist to moviegoing in the Gadsden area took place—the first drive-in theater opened in Etowah County.

The drive-in theater was the invention of Richard M. Hollingshead Jr., who came up with the idea of an outdoor theater where people could watch a movie from the comfort of their own car. The first drive-in was built in Camden, New Jersey, by a group of investors at a cost of $30,000 in 1933, and the first movie was shown there on June 6 of that year. Admission to this new type of theatre was 25¢ per person with a maximum admission of $1 per car. Through the years, this type of theater grew in popularity. In 1943, there were 820 listed in the United States. Within the next 10 years, that number increased to more than 4,000.

The first drive-in to open in Gadsden was the Tower Drive-In Theatre on U.S. 431 near the present site of Public Wholesale, close to the Gadsden-Glencoe city limits. The Tower opened on October 2, 1947, and was in operation until late 1956. This theater was

Gadsden's Pitman Theatre is shown here on opening night, September 26, 1947.

The Rainbow Drive-In Theatre opened in September 1952. (Courtesy of the C.S. Pitman family.)

a popular place, and the idea of watching a movie from the comfort of one's own car was catching on quickly. A second drive-in theater, the Grove Drive-In Theatre, opened in July 1949 in the Alabama City area and was in operation until 1957.

The popularity of these open-air theaters caught on quickly. Families loaded up the car and went to the Tower or the Grove to see a double or triple feature. This type of theater was inexpensive because one could take his/her own popcorn, candy, and soft drinks to save money or could visit the snack bar for everything from hot dogs and barbecues to ice cream and candy. Teens loved the drive-in because it was an inexpensive night out and the challenge of sneaking in was too great to pass up. Many teenagers during this era slipped into the movies in the trunk of a friend's car.

Many things are fondly remembered by the people who went to these early drive-ins. Upon entering the driveway, one would pull up to the ticket booth. This was a place to also buy popcorn. After paying, the moviegoer drove around and picked a good spot from the several hundred parking spaces. A speaker was hanging on a post that the driver would reach out and place on his/her window. Many of these drive-in speakers were "accidentally" brought home as a souvenir from the show.

The local drive-ins all had great snack bars, and most people visited them before the movie started. Most drive-ins offered a double feature, cartoons, and short subjects. Seats were also available at the front of the snack bar if a person wanted to sit outside and watch the movies.

Ward Wright was the owner and operator of both the Tower and Grove Drive-In Theatres during their years of operation in Gadsden. Wright had enjoyed such success with his first two theaters that plans were underway to open a third one on Highway 278, near the Gadsden–Hokes Bluff city limits. The Ranch W Drive-In opened on July 19, 1952, on the Piedmont Highway. In September 1952, another new drive-in was nearing completion on Rainbow Drive in Gadsden. This large drive-in was built and operated by C.S. Pitman, the owner of the Pitman Theatre, located on Broad Street in Gadsden.

The decade of the 1940s saw rapid growth in many areas in Gadsden, and several local landmarks slowly faded into history. One such landmark that was lost during the latter days of the 1940s was the beautiful Elliott home on Forrest Avenue. This elegant mansion at 818 Forrest Avenue was originally built by William and Susan Christopher. Colonel R.B. Kyle purchased this property during the 1860s, at a time when Gadsden was beginning to grow from a small village into a thriving city. The Kyle family lived in this home until it was given to Nena, the Kyles' oldest daughter, in 1897. This house was remodeled by Captain James M. Elliott Jr. and Nena Kyle Elliott into one of Gadsden's most recognizable residences.

The Elliotts totally renovated the house, adding a third story, a greenhouse, a conservatory, a gazebo, a carriage house, and a stable. The carriage house was later used as the first Little Theatre of Gadsden because it provided ample room for a stage as well as room to seat many theater patrons. This ornate house was the Elliott home until the late 1940s, at which time the house and 4 acres of land were placed on the market.

Etowah County was planning to build a new courthouse, and plans were also being made to move the site of the seat of the county government. For this purpose, the Elliott property was purchased by the county in October 1946 for $140,000. The house was torn down in April 1948 to make way for the new courthouse.

The Elliott home is shown here just before it was demolished to make room for the present Etowah County Courthouse.

The construction of the new courthouse was not without controversy. The old courthouse was sold to a Boston concern for $200,000. A dispute over the purchase of the Elliott property and the sale of the old courthouse held up construction of the new courthouse for some time until the Alabama Supreme Court ruled that the board of revenue had the authority to sell the old courthouse. This action cleared the way for the erection of the present Etowah County Courthouse. The million-dollar structure was completed in 1950.

The new Etowah County Courthouse was built on Forrest Avenue between Eighth and Ninth Streets and served as the home of the county government as well as the county jail. This was a welcome new home for the jail because the old county jail was in very poor condition.

Several homes on Forrest Avenue slowly began to disappear as this street became part of the downtown business district. The Kyle home, the Standifer home, the Lay home, and the Paden home soon faded into the pages of the history books just as the beautiful Elliott home had. Gadsden lost these landmarks, but had gained a modern courthouse.

In 1951, demolition began on the old Etowah County Courthouse building. Over the next few months, Etowah County residents watched as this downtown landmark was slowly reduced to a vacant lot. The demolition was completed in May 1951. Another item of interest from 1951 was that the Magna Carta oak tree was transplanted to the west side of the new courthouse location.

Gadsden suffered other growing pains during the early 1950s. One major problem that needed immediate attention was the increased automobile traffic across Memorial Bridge. This two-lane bridge was having severe overcrowding problems and a second traffic bridge was becoming necessary.

Construction is underway on the Meighan Bridge across the Coosa River in this photo.

The problem was corrected when a new bridge spanning the Coosa River was dedicated on December 18, 1954. The first step in addressing the situation had actually taken place several years before, during the administration of J. Herbert Meighan, the late mayor of Gadsden. The structure was 1,056 feet from east to west and 70 feet wide. The four traffic lanes were 13 feet wide with a 4-foot median strip separating the four lanes. Pedestrians crossing the bridge had a 6-foot walkway on each side.

On December 18, 1954, the bridge was officially dedicated with Mary Spence Meighan and Lynn C. Meighan, granddaughters of the late mayor, cutting the ribbon to open the bridge to traffic. A short ceremony was held in a brisk, cold wind with Congressman Albert Rains delivering the dedicatory address. Following the speech by Rains, Governor-elect James E. "Big Jim" Folsom was introduced and spoke briefly on his association with Mayor Meighan. The wife of the late mayor and her son J. Herbert Meighan Jr. were given the seats of honor on the speakers' platform. The first vehicle to officially cross the new bridge was the Meighan automobile carrying Mrs. Meighan.

At this time, the Meighan Bridge was the most expensive bridge built across a stream or river in the history of the state of Alabama. The bridge was constructed by the C.F. Rule Company of Nashville, Tennessee. In conjunction with the opening of the bridge, the new four-lane approaches, reaching from Third Street in East Gadsden to Ninth Street on the west side of the bridge, were also opened.

Although the Meighan Boulevard project took several more years to complete, it had, even in its early stages, done much to reduce the traffic load formerly carried by the old river bridge. When completed, Meighan Boulevard was a four-lane roadway from Attalla to the eastern city limits with tie-ins on the Piedmont and Anniston Highways, and it proved to be important in relieving traffic congestion in the Gadsden area.

While many changes in the 1950s brought better times to the Gadsden area, some events signalled a slow down in the local economy. Two such changes were the closings of Gadsden's largest employers. The Standard-Coosa Thatcher Company's Sauquoit plant closed in 1956, and the Dwight plant of Cone Mills closed in 1959.

In 1927, the Sauquoit Spinning Company, a yarn manufacturer employing over 300 workers, began operation on North Eighth Street near the foot of Lookout Mountain. In 1930, this mill was sold to the Coosa-Thatcher Company of Chattanooga, Tennessee. The company generated thousands of dollars for the tax coffers each year, much of it on the city and county levels. When the decision was reached to close the Gadsden plant, a financial blow was felt by the entire community. For many family breadwinners, the closure meant long months of unemployment.

Many former employees were unable to find work and were forced to leave the Gadsden area. For many of these unemployed workers who had been making above-average wages, the heartbreak of losing their means of support was a nightmare that went on for months and months. Gadsden was still feeling the effects of the mill's closing in April 1959 when another jolt hit the local economy.

Cone Mills closed the Dwight Manufacturing Company during a labor dispute and ensuing strike during the months of March and April in 1959. The Dwight Manufacturing Company had been built in Alabama City in 1895. The company, originally from Chicopee, Massachusetts, built their large textile mill on a 30-acre tract in the small town

The closing of the Standard-Coosa Thatcher Company's Sauquoit Mill in 1956 was a jolt to the Gadsden economy.

Machinery is being removed from the Cone Mill in Alabama City following the decision to close the giant textile mill.

that had been founded with the hope of attracting industry to the Etowah County area. The original building, along with several additions, was one of the largest cotton mills in the United States; it covered more than 957,000 square feet. At the height of its operation in 1953, the textile giant employed more than 2,600 people.

Through the years, the Dwight Manufacturing Company was famous for their manufacture of a grade of cloth known as Cabot A. This cloth sheeting was considered some of the finest available and was shipped throughout the world.

Dwight Mill merged with Cone Mills in March 1951. The mill continued to operate and be a major employer until March 18, 1959, when a labor dispute and strike halted production at the mill. The dispute between management and labor was never fully resolved and the decision was made to close the Alabama City mill. A few days following the decision to close the Dwight Manufacturing Company, large trucks began hauling equipment from the premises. This giant building was then used as a warehouse for the next 20 years.

The 1950s also saw the end of an era come in Gadsden when the once beautiful Gadsden Theatre closed its doors for good. The Gadsden Theatre had been a downtown landmark since its construction in 1908. Known originally as the Hayden-Pake Theatre, the auditorium had been the scene of countless live productions, vaudeville, and motion pictures for many years. The very popular Gadsden Theatre had undergone renovations and name changes in its attempts to compete with the Princess Theatre and later the

Above, the Gadsden Theatre is being torn down. This local landmark closed its doors on October 31, 1954.

Pitman Theatre. By the early 1950s, the Gadsden Theatre was beginning to show its age and its interior became more and more run down.

The Gadsden Theatre closed its doors forever following a double feature on October 31, 1954. The final features shown at this grand theater were *Anybody Seen My Girl* and *Ivory Hunter*. The theater stood dark and vacant until 1958, when the structure was demolished to make room for the drive-in tellers and parking lot of the American National Bank.

Although the 1950s saw the destruction of the Gadsden Theatre, two new theaters also opened in Gadsden during this period: the Bama Theatre on Forrest Avenue and the Carver Theatre on North Sixth Street. The movies at the Bama Theatre, managed by Thomas Gentry, changed every three days, and this theater was a very popular place with children living in Alabama City. Westerns were a specialty on Saturday mornings at the Bama. A young moviegoer could see a full-length feature, a cartoon, and a newsreel there during the 1950s. A skating rink was later located in the Bama Theatre building.

The Carver Theatre opened on North Sixth Street in downtown Gadsden and replaced the Gem Theatre, which had been in operation a few doors down during the 1940s. The Carver showed the most popular movies and offered the finest in entertainment to the local black community. Harold T. Spears was the manager of the Carver Theatre during the 1950s.

The Capitol Theatre, located at 516 Broad Street, closed its doors during the 1950s. A downtown tradition since the late 1920s, the Capitol specialized in Westerns. The lady who sold tickets at the Capitol always wore red and was long remembered as the "lady in red." By the end of the 1950s, the downtown Gadsden area had only the Princess, Pitman, and Carver Theatres competing for the moviegoer's attention and dollars. The Ritz Theatre was the only theater located in the Alabama City area following the closing of the Bama Theatre.

In 1961, a new form of entertainment took the Gadsden area by storm. This was the year that a professional football game came to town and the Gadsden Raiders made their debut. The Gadsden entry into the Dixie Professional Football League was made up of former college football players as well as several local stars. All of the Gadsden Raiders' home games were played at Etowah Stadium in Attalla. Players were paid an average of $25 per game. Jimmy Pettus, a former Auburn University standout, led a team that was loaded with local talent, including Terrell Wallen, Gary O'Steen, Buster Gross, Terry Harris, and Charles Ledbetter. This was Gadsden's first try at professional football.

The season opened on September 9, 1961 with the Raiders earning a hard-fought, 21-6 win over the Montgomery Confederates. The following week, the Raiders defeated the Selma Falcons, 23-6. The third week, the Raiders traveled to Birmingham and destroyed the Vulcans, 40-6. During their first season the Raiders lost only one game (to Montgomery) while posting seven wins.

By virtue of the Raiders' 1961 record, the team was awarded the Dixie Professional Football League's championship and the honor of hosting the All-Star game, which was played on November 12, 1961, at Etowah Stadium. The game featured the Gadsden Raiders playing a team made up of the top stars from the other teams in the league. The

Pictured here in 1961 are members of the Gadsden Raiders, including Gil Evans, Melton Burgess, Bill Prestridge, and Gary O'Steen.

league trophy was presented to Johnny Lynch, one of the Raiders' owners, at halftime by Commissioner Virgil Pierson.

The Raiders overcame an early 6-0 deficit to win the game at 20-6 going into the final quarter. Pettus led the Raiders' offense, bringing the 5,000 fans to their feet several times. Melton Burgess was also one of the game's stars, along with Terrell Wallen and Gary O'Steen. An ex-Auburn halfback, Pettus tallied the Raiders first points just before halftime with an 80-yard run. The score at the half was knotted at 6-6. The Raiders scored two second-half touchdowns to take a 20-6 lead before the all-stars made their gallant comeback, fighting to a 20-20 tie.

Following the All-Star game, the Gadsden Raiders defeated a team from Atlanta 37-6 to improve their record to eight wins, one loss, and one tie. The following week, the Raiders played host to the Dothan Colts. The Colts were one of the South's stronger gridiron teams, having gone undefeated the two prior seasons.

The Dothan squad made the trip to Attalla to face their stiffest challenge in two years, and the Colts, behind the passing of quarterback Rosey Ryan, handed the Raiders their second loss in their inaugural season. The Colts started the scoring on their first possession of the night. Dothan quarterback Ryan passed 5 yards to Mike Palmer to cap a 9-play, 64-yard drive. Billy Gilbert added the extra point, giving the Colts a 7-0 lead. Gadsden tied the score with just over 12 minutes to go in the game. The Raiders' touchdown drive covered 10 yards in three plays, with Terrell Wallen scoring on a 2-yard run. Gary O'Steen added the extra point for a 7-7 score. In the closing minutes of the game, Ryan once again threw a pass for the go-ahead score and a 14-7 win.

For four years, the Gadsden Raiders fielded a competitive team. Many local athletes wore the Raider uniform and brought good football to the Gadsden area.

The downtown Gadsden movie theaters continued to be the places to go for good entertainment during the 1960s. The competition between the managers of the Princess and the Pitman Theatres had reached an unbelievable pitch by 1963. The Pitman Theatre offered a kiddie show on Saturday mornings during the summer months and a full house was expected each week. These shows were sponsored by the Royal Crown Bottling Company, and admission to this kiddie show was six R.C. bottle caps. On more than one occasion, Cousin Cliff Holman entertained the large crowd of young people at the R.C. Kiddie Show.

On April 5, 1963, the Pitman Theatre was the scene of a Hollywood-type premier. The theater, along with the entire city, rolled out the red carpet to welcome the two young stars of the movie *To Kill a Mockingbird*. This movie actually premiered in Birmingham,

Phillip Alford and Mary Badham are welcomed to a Hollywood-type premier of To Kill a Mockingbird.

although Phillip Alford, who played the role of "Jem," was a former Gadsden resident, and this event was planned for him and Mary Badham, who played the role of "Scout."

The guests of honor arrived at the Pitman with a police escort at 7:15 p.m. Broad Street was blocked off between Sixth and Seventh Streets to accommodate the large crowd who had gathered to see the movie stars. Gadsden Mayor Les Gilliland presented the two guests of honor with keys to the city before the movie feature began, and Lieutenant Governor James Allen made a presentation making the two youngsters honorary members of the state senate. Following the movie, the stars were available to greet hundreds of fans and sign autographs.

The movie was nominated for eight Academy Awards. Badham was nominated for best supporting actress in this movie version of Harper Lee's Pulitzer Prize–winning novel. Gregory Peck took top honors as best actor, while the movie won a total of three Oscars.

The fierce competition between the Pitman and Princess Theatres came to an end on Monday night, November 4, 1963. This Monday night was a usual night at the movies. A small crowd of less than 100 people were enjoying the movie *All the Way Home*. The movie ended around 10:30 p.m., and the theater closed its doors for what would be the last time in this grand theater's long life.

At 10:48 p.m., Gadsden police officer Bill O'Bryant was walking his beat downtown when he noticed what appeared to be a garbage can burning next to the theater. O'Bryant turned in the alarm and several fire engines answered the call from the downtown Central Fire Station. When the first trucks arrived on the scene, they found the theater totally engulfed in flames.

Gadsden's Princess Theatre is pictured here engulfed in the flames of a late-night fire. The theatre was destroyed on November 4, 1963.

The firemen battled the flames into the night and early morning hours. It appeared for a while that the entire block would be lost, although the fire was finally contained to only the theater. Several nearby businesses, however, received extensive water and smoke damage. By daybreak the next morning, the once beautiful Princess Theatre had been gutted and reduced to smoldering embers. The flames had burned completely through the roof, and water was standing almost 6 feet deep at the front of the theater.

The charred remains of the Princess Theatre were knocked down shortly thereafter. One of Gadsden's most beautiful landmarks was now gone. The Princess Theatre had ended its place in Gadsden's history on a cold November night in 1963.

In the 1960s, several new buildings were constructed in the Gadsden area. The Baptist Memorial Hospital was a new structure that increased the bed space as well as the services offered by the hospital. A new library was also constructed on College Street in May 1964. This was soon followed by the demolition of Gadsden's Carnegie Library. The Gadsden Technical Junior College opened its doors to students for the first time in September 1965.

The Baptist Memorial Hospital had been faced with the need for a newer and more modern facility for some time. A contract for the construction of this new medical facility was awarded on May 30, 1961, and the construction was actually completed some 28 months later. The new hospital was erected on a 20-acre tract of land located in East Gadsden near the Goodyear Tire and Rubber Company. The low bidder on the $2.5-million project was Memphis, Tennessee contractor Robert C. Crouch and Company, who outbid other firms from Tennessee, Georgia, Alabama, and Florida.

A citizens group had been organized to raise $1 million to begin the construction of the planned 200-bed, 6-story hospital. An additional $2 million was received in federal funds for the project. Local businessman Ira Phillips headed the Baptist Hospital campaign

The Baptist Memorial Hospital is shown here under construction in 1963. The hospital opened on September 29, 1963.

The new Gadsden Public Library opened on College Street on June 28, 1964.

drive. An open house was held at the new hospital on September 29, 1963, and over 10,000 people toured the facility. The dedication of the new Baptist Memorial Hospital was held the following day.

On June 28, 1964, Gadsden's new public library was dedicated and opened to the public. This library was constructed at 254 College Street on the old Striplin School property. The City of Gadsden had been awarded an Accelerated Public Works Grant of $272,000 to match city money for the construction of the building. Roberts Brothers was awarded the contract to build the structure with a base bid of $503,331, and the new library was ready in only 12 months. The 39,000-square-foot building had room for 200,000 books and was designated as a federal depository for the government documents of Congressman Albert Rains, who lived in Gadsden.

In 1965, a giant step was taken in education in the Gadsden area when the Gadsden Technical Junior College opened in September. The junior college was one of 12 built in Alabama at this time to serve the needs of youth, as well as adults, in the local area. The institution was under the supervision of the State Board of Education and by the Southern Association of Schools and Colleges.

The Gadsden Technical Junior College was built on a 115-acre site in East Gadsden on property adjacent to the Alabama School of Trades. The first phase of construction included the administration building, science building, library, student center, and fine arts building. Future plans included the construction of an engineering building, additional classrooms, and several other structures.

Allan D. Naylor served as the first president of the new Gadsden Technical Junior College, and the first two faculty appointments at the new institution were Joe Ronald Johnson, who taught English and speech, and Mrs. Sarah S. Massey, who taught history. The first year's enrollment was 750 students.

Probably the greatest single change to come to the Gadsden area during the 1960s grew from the Civil Rights Movement. Inequality existed in all phases of life, from hiring practices to voting rights. Blacks were even required to ride in the back of local buses. This was challenged on a Montgomery bus when Rosa Parks refused to comply with the discriminatory practice, an event that brought about the beginning of the Civil Rights Movement in the South.

The Civil Rights Movement, which began during the 1950s, slowly gathered momentum, and by the next decade's end, led to many changes in the everyday lives of people. Before the Civil Rights Movement, racial segregation was widespread in the United States, particularly in the South. The school systems were segregated, with whites and blacks attending separate schools. Everything throughout society was segregated, from waiting rooms to water fountains. Although blacks and whites attended the same movie theaters, the black movie patrons were required to enter and exit through a separate entrance.

Under the leadership of individuals such as Q.D. Adams, efforts in Gadsden drew national attention. The Reverend Martin Luther King Jr. made several trips to Gadsden during this time to further the cause and to keep national attention on the area. The news media focused on the Gadsden area so much that actors Paul Newman and Marlon Brando came to the city. During these visits, changes were made because of the attention that these actors and others brought to the movement.

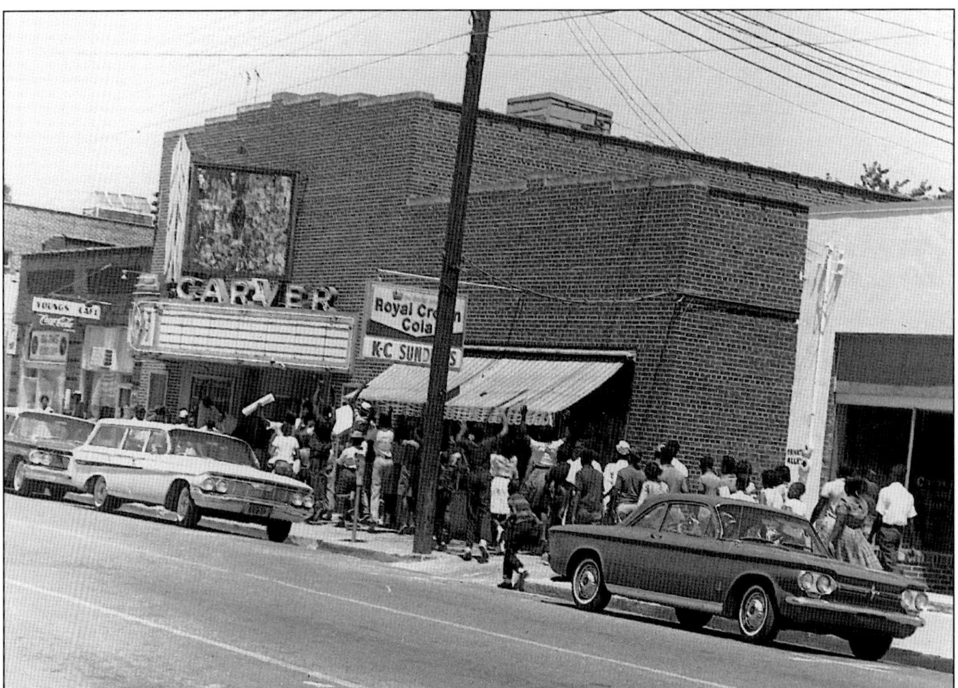

A crowd of civil rights protesters gather in front of the Carver Theatre to march to the Etowah County Courthouse.

Hazel Brannon Smith, a Gadsden native, won the Pulitzer Prize for journalism in 1964.

Several marches were organized by Adams and his followers in Gadsden. Groups gathered at one of the local churches or at the Carver Theatre and went on to the Etowah County Courthouse. The demonstrators were often surrounded by state troopers, sheriff's deputies, and city police, who ordered them to turn around and disband after reaching the courthouse. Adams, at this point, led the marchers back to the church.

The protest marches in the downtown Gadsden area were relatively peaceful, although there were several instances in which state troopers were accused of using cattle prods to break up the marchers. Although these Civil Rights demonstrations were somewhat peaceful here as compared to the violence in Birmingham and other large cities, the impact was felt throughout the nation.

A former Gadsden resident Hazel Brannon Smith played a pivotal role during the movement. She graduated from Gadsden High School in 1930 and later attended the University of Alabama. Upon her graduation from college, she went into the newspaper business in Mississippi. During the 1950s, when the Civil Rights Movement garnered national attention, Smith took up the cause of a black man who had been shot by a local sheriff. Smith ran editorials concerning this unprovoked attack, and because of her editorials, she was faced with a huge libel suit. The Supreme Court dismissed this suit, and Hazel Brannon Smith was later awarded a Pulitzer Prize for journalism in 1964.

During the 1960s, great strides were made to break down the barriers that had existed between the black and white communities. Through government legislation, voting irregularities were corrected and hiring practices in the government and private sector were addressed. Barriers affecting everyday activities, such as segregated restaurants, theaters, public transportation, and waiting rooms, also began to fall away. The public school system was desegregated in the late 1960s, leading to the closing of several Gadsden schools and the consolidation of others.

9. The Turbulent Seventies

The different decades of the twentieth century have seen Gadsden going through many changes. In times of war, Gadsden has sent her sons and daughters into foreign lands to defend the freedom that every American holds dear. Gadsden has witnessed times of severe depression and has celebrated the heyday of Hollywood and the growth of local movie theaters. The popularity of drive-in theaters and restaurants grew at a rapid rate in the decades of the 1950s and 1960s. In the 1960s, the United States became more and more involved in a very unpopular war in Southeast Asia. By the end of this decade, hundreds of U.S. troops were deployed and facing combat in Vietnam.

In the 1970s, more attention was placed on the war in Southeast Asia. The related unrest at home was growing and was marked by student protests denouncing America's involvement. Things came to a head during the presidential election of 1972. A peace accord was reached between North Vietnam and South Vietnam, bringing the fighting to a end. But following the removal of American military forces, the fighting resumed, and North Vietnam slowly overthrew the weaker country to the south.

News on the local scene during the 1970s included a destructive fire that gutted Gadsden High School in November 1972. The school was rebuilt amid much controversy. Another important event, the opening of the Gadsden Mall marked a large exodus of retail merchants from Broad Street and downtown.

During this decade, a new mayor was elected. Steve Means, a former band director at Disque Junior High School, would hold this position every term except one since 1974.

The Gadsden Civic Theatre grew and eventually purchased the old Ritz Theatre to house its productions. The first multi-screen theaters opened in the Gadsden area in the 1970s.

Former University of Alabama football star John Croyle had a dream of opening a home for young people who needed a second chance. The former Gadsden Tiger and Crimson Tide standout used his talents following college to build his home for boys near Southside. The Big Oak Boy's Ranch and later the Girl's Ranch near Springville have given many young people another chance to make something of their lives.

The decade of the 1970s heralded many changes in the Gadsden area. A period of unrest settled over the area because of events happening both locally and nationally, but by the end of this decade, improved services offered to the residents of Gadsden propelled the city into the twenty-first century and into winning an "All-America City" designation.

One of the major news events of the 1970s occurred on May 2, 1972. It was on this date that record numbers of Etowah County voters went to the polls for a special referendum. The residents of a dry county once again stood at the crossroads of whether to stay "dry" or vote "wet" and legalize the sale of alcoholic beverages. In former wet-dry referendums in Etowah County, voters had chosen to retain prohibition. The last time such an election had taken place was 1968. At that time, Etowah County had been dry for almost 30 years.

To get a new referendum, petitions had to be circulated and enough registered voters had to sign to require a new vote. As these petitions circulated, it became obvious that this vote would be a lot closer than votes in the past. Opponents on both sides of the issue were taking an active part in the referendum.

Several issues came out in this campaign, such as the added revenue for education and local projects that could be raised through the taxation of alcohol. Additional jobs were also promised throughout the Etowah County area. One major issue was the age-old problem of moonshiners and bootleggers, but the legalization of alcohol promised to put these people out of business. "White lightning" had been made in secluded areas for years and the shutting down of illegal stills was an ongoing problem for the Etowah County Sheriff's Department.

The illegal sale of beer, wine, and whiskey was happening throughout Gadsden and the remote parts of the county. Raids carried out by local law enforcement officers netted

Sheriff's deputies prepare to smash "white lightning" in front of Etowah County Courthouse.

large amounts of untaxed alcohol that would be smashed and poured out in the gutter at the Etowah County Courthouse and the Gadsden City Hall. Much of these bootleggers' business was to underage customers. One major selling point in this referendum was that these two major problems would be taken resolved.

When the day of the vote arrived, it was obvious that the outcome was going to be extremely close. In fact, the future of Gadsden and Etowah County on this issue was decided by less than 1,000 votes. The final tally showed 14,979 people voting "wet" and 14,289 voting "dry." The final margin of victory stood at just 690 votes. The "wet" victory was attained by adding to the 1968 city margin and cutting into "dry" forces in the county. Attalla voted about the same in 1968 as it did in 1972—in fact, there was a change of only 16 votes.

The licensing procedure that enabled Etowah County to have legal sales of alcohol began as soon as official certification of the vote was sent to Montgomery. The Etowah County Commission also had to set license levies for all retailers. Shortly after these were in place, officials from the Alabama Alcoholic Beverage Control Board came to the area for public meetings to explain the board's program to the city and county officials and to accept applications for licenses.

Also in 1972, two other Alabama counties voted to go wet. Dale and Conecuh Counties joined Etowah as "wet," bringing the total to 35 of Alabama's 67 counties.

During the 1970s, a new road opened through the Gadsden area. On September 15, 1972, this 2.8-mile section of Highway 411 was dedicated and opened along the Coosa River in Gadsden. Named in honor of Albert Rains, a longtime Gadsden resident and former member of the U.S. House of Representatives, this $3.5-million stretch of roadway ran through the area once known as Riverside Park and connected Ewing Avenue to Rainbow Drive.

The project began on June 18, 1970, and was completed on August 18, 1972. This scenic stretch of highway runs under three bridges—the Memorial Bridge, the railroad trestle, and the Meighan Bridge, all of which are in close proximity. The west end of the railroad trestle was rebuilt to eliminate the wooden supports, which were replaced with a steel span under the tracks upheld by concrete pillars.

One section of this new highway reached into the Coosa River at one point near Convention Hall, where tons of quarry stone, or rip-rap, were hauled in to build the road bed. Reinforced concrete culverts were used to span two inlets on the boulevard. The inlet water from the Coosa River was drained, the road bed and culverts constructed, and then the water was allowed to re-enter the inlet.

On the south end, the boulevard swings from Rainbow Drive south of Riverview Regional Medical Center, formerly known as the Holy Name of Jesus Hospital, and then skirts the Coosa River. The northern end is on Ewing Avenue near Tidmore Bend Road, or Princeton Avenue. The new boulevard cuts several minutes of driving time for north- and south-bound traffic, serving as a bypass from congested city streets.

Following the dedication and ribbon cutting for the new highway, a luncheon was held in honor of Mr. and Mrs. Rains. The festivities were a fitting tribute to a country boy from Sand Mountain who achieved national prominence as a master orator, a state and federal legislator, and finally, a prime mover in the modern lawmaking process.

Allison Rains cuts the ribbon for the new Albert Rains Boulevard. The retired U.S. representative and Gadsden mayor Les Gilliland look on. (Courtesy of the Rains family.)

A native of Grove Oak, Rains was born March 11, 1902, to Elbert Rains and Louella Campbell Rains. The new addition to the family was named Albert after his father's twin brother. After attending the public schools in Dekalb County, Albert entered Snead Seminary in Boaz, and after a two-year stay, he taught school in Jackson County. At age 20, Rains was named principal of Pisgah High School.

In 1925, he returned to school and enrolled at the Jacksonville State Normal School. He later attended the University of Alabama, where he earned a bachelor's degree. In 1928, he passed the state bar exam with one of the highest scores recorded at that time. Rains moved to the Gadsden area, where he began to practice law first as a criminal lawyer and later as a circuit solicitor.

In 1942, Rains was elected to the state legislature. Among his many accomplishments during his brief stay in Montgomery was co-authoring the bill to establish a dental school at the University of Alabama in Birmingham. In May 1944, the young lawmaker achieved his lifelong ambition when he was elected to represent the U.S. Fifth Congressional District in the 79th Congress.

During his career in Washington, Rains helped write numerous housing and urban renewal programs, which included the nursing home program, public housing for low-income families, and most of the new laws on banking and savings and loan association practices. Rains served in Congress during the administration of five different presidents before his retirement on January 3, 1965.

While the 1970s saw many new and improved services coming to the city of Gadsden, this decade also experienced one of the largest fires to hit the area in many years. One of the city's largest schools sustained major damage from the fire and caused an interruption of classes in November 1972.

On November 9, 1972, things seemed to be normal for a Thursday afternoon at Gadsden High School. Most attention was on the 24th annual Charity Bowl, which was scheduled for the following evening between cross-town rivals Gadsden High School and Emma Sansom High School. As the school day was drawing to a close, several students thought they noticed the smell of smoke in the school's auditorium. No evidence was found to indicate that anything was wrong and school was dismissed at 3:00 p.m. as usual. This was the last time that this grand old building closed its doors. A few short hours later, Gadsden High School was changed forever.

The call came in at 4:55 p.m. to Gadsden's Central Fire Station. A neighbor noticed what appeared to be smoke coming from the auditorium of the school and turned in the alarm. When the first units arrived, they found the auditorium engulfed in flames. The fire quickly spread throughout the structure until the entire main building was

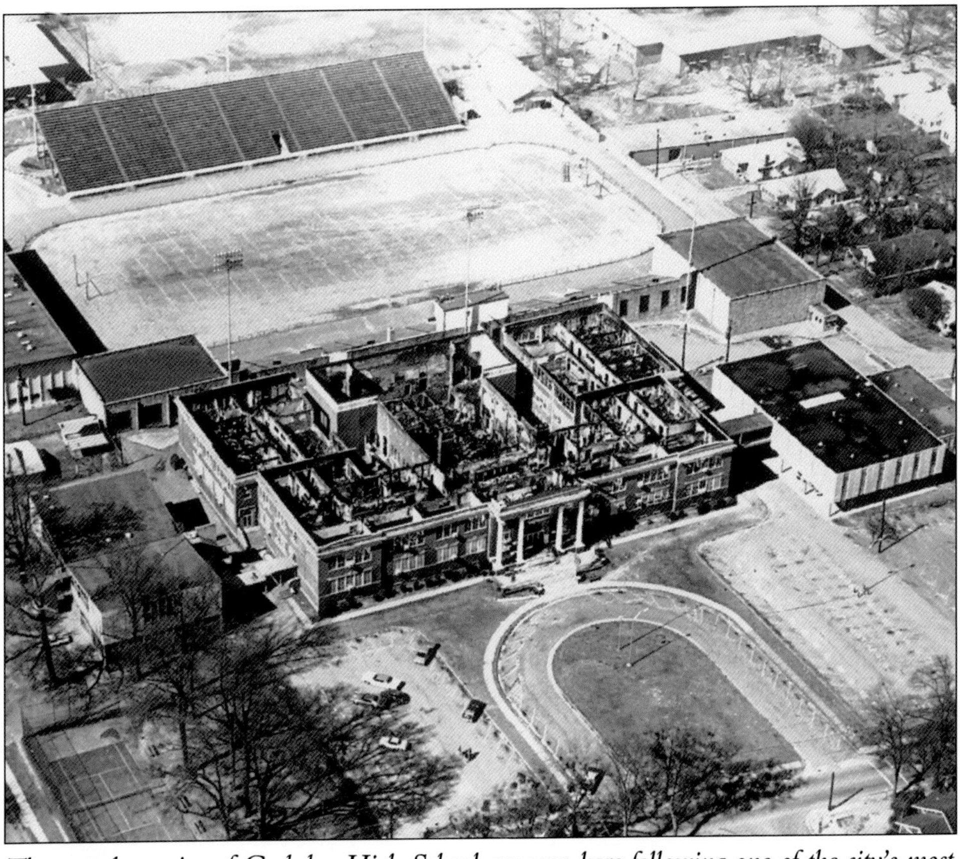

The gutted remains of Gadsden High School are seen here following one of the city's most destructive fires.

a blazing inferno. All Gadsden firefighting equipment was called in, although the fire was already out of control when the first truck arrived. The call went out for help to the surrounding towns and communities, with most responding. Firefighting equipment was sent to Gadsden from throughout Etowah and surrounding counties. A snorkel unit was sent from Jacksonville, and the Birmingham Fire Department was put on standby.

Gadsden firemen laid miles of hose with every piece of equipment available in Gadsden at the scene. The Gadsden Fire Department was aided by units from Glencoe, Southside, Ashville, Jacksonville, Steele, Ragland, and several other towns. Attalla and Rainbow City sent units to Gadsden to cover the city in case any other fires broke out during this long night. Gadsden police, Civil Defense, Etowah County Rescue Squad, and others aided in handling traffic and the crowd.

Early in the night, the situation appeared to be a lost cause. Firemen and many volunteers battled gallantly and succeeded in keeping the blaze from spreading to adjoining buildings. The two modern annex buildings separated by walkways were saved and sustained no damage. The main building, however, was almost a total loss. The interior was a gutted shell.

Thousands of spectators watched the 49-year-old building go up in smoke. At the time of the fire, 1,500 students were enrolled at the school. Several units of the Gadsden Fire Department remained on the scene the following morning with readied hoses. Fifty-six off-duty firemen were called in to assist in fighting this huge blaze. Luckily, no one was injured during the night-long ordeal.

Classes resumed in the remaining buildings on November 20. The girl's and boy's gym and the field house were used for classrooms, and physical education classes were suspended. Wooden partitions were built in the gyms and classes were held in shifts. A morning shift of four classes and an afternoon shift were held. The lunchroom, band room, and choral room were also used to hold classes. Furniture was salvaged from classrooms on the first floor of the school.

Despite this destructive fire, the Charity Bowl football game was played as scheduled. The entrances to Murphree Stadium nearest the burned out building were roped off, with spectators having to enter from the west side of the stadium.

This blaze was one of the city's worst fires judging by the amount of property damage that resulted, and an insurance settlement set the value of the loss at $1.28 million. One of the amazing things about this fire was that classes were only interrupted for six days.

The rebuilding of the school was completed by Thompson Construction Company of Gadsden. At first, the building was thought to be a total loss, although a later survey of the damage revealed that much of the burned-out structure could be rebuilt. The only real casualty of the fire was the school's auditorium, which, it was later determined, would not be rebuilt.

Throughout the spring and summer of 1973, work continued on the main structure. As the summer began to draw to a close, it was obvious that the school would not be ready to open by the first of September.

When the day came for the opening of classes for the 1973–1974 school year, a decision had to be made. Tentative plans called for classes to open only when the school was

The new Gadsden High School was rebuilt on the burned-out shell of the original building.

completed and the time missed would be made up during the following summer. Classes finally began in mid-October in the rebuilt Gadsden High School. A new format for classes greeted the students upon the opening of the school; the open concept and team teaching had replaced the smaller classrooms. These larger classes were taught by two or more teachers working as a team.

With June approaching, the first school year in the new building was coming to a close. The Class of 1974 held its commencement exercises in Murphree Stadium on a hot evening in early July. By mid-summer, classes had concluded for the 1973–1974 school term. Things would be back to normal by September 1974. A lot had happened in just a few short months in the life of Gadsden High School. From a devastating fire in November 1972 to a completely remodeled school, the student body of Gadsden's largest high school had endured much.

The 1970s proved to be a record-setting decade for destructive fires in the Gadsden area. Estimates for 1973 alone exceeded $3.5 million, and residents were feeling the need for improved fire protection. Most of the firefighting equipment in service at the time had been purchased between the years of 1952 and 1959. These trucks were now inadequate and outdated, a fact that had been proven at the disastrous Gadsden High School fire.

Public Safety Commissioner Bill Perry made a promise to the residents of Gadsden to upgrade the fire department. The City began to purchase new firefighting equipment and to take outdated fire engines out of service in July 1973 following the arrival of a new American LaFrance 100-foot aerial truck. The fire engine was purchased at a cost of $109,830 and replaced a 1955 model, 85-foot ladder truck that was traded in. The final cost was reduced to $99,830 after the trade-in.

Gadsden added a new fire engine, a 100-foot aerial ladder truck, in the 1970s.

The new ladder truck was stationed at the Central Fire Station until the city's new snorkel-type truck with a 90-foot elevated platform arrived in November 1973. The snorkel and the new ladder truck gave Gadsden enough aerial ladder coverage to meet all the requirements within the city. The next two pieces of firefighting equipment that arrived were pumper-ladder units, one of which was placed in East Gadsden and the other in West Gadsden. This type of truck, which carried additional ladders, gave the city more coverage in residential areas. Two other pumpers arrived the following spring—one was stationed downtown and the other in Alabama City.

The first six fire engines purchased by the City represented a total investment of more than $600,000. During the next several year, other pieces of equipment were purchased to gradually update the department. Many other improvements were also made to enhance the city's fire protection. More and better training also became an important element in improving fire protection in the city.

The City also started a fire medic program that provided emergency medical service throughout the Gadsden area. An outdated firetruck was repainted white and equipped as the first fire medic unit operating out of the Central Fire Station. Today, the City of Gadsden has one of the most modern and best-equipped fire departments in the state.

Another major topic of interest in the Gadsden area during the 1970s was local politics, and the year 1974 was one of the most interesting in recent times. Mayor Les Gilliland, who had served as Gadsden's mayor for the previous 11 years, had resigned his office earlier to pursue other interests; C.B. "Red" Collier Jr. finished Gilliland's unexpired term.

The early frontrunners for the office of mayor appeared to be former Gadsden City Commissioner Hoyt Warsham and local businessman Bebo Klyce. A newcomer to the political arena was Disque Junior High School band director Steve Means, who at the time of the election was only 28 years old. At first, Means was considered a longshot in the race with Warsham and Klyce. Other prominent names on the ballot included Chester Hicks and Robert Avery.

Hoyt Warsham was attempting a political comeback in this election. In 1970, he ran for re-election as public works commissioner and lost to George Sizemore by a 2-to-1 margin. Now, a short four years later, Warsham appeared to be the frontrunner for the city's highest office.

Election day fell on May 8, 1974, and found Warsham pulling in 32 percent of the vote. Much of Warsham's support came in the Alabama City boxes, as had been expected. Many of his 5,106 votes came from his home territory. The biggest surprise of the election was Warsham's opponent in the June 4th runoff.

Political newcomer Steve Means had finished a strong second, polling 3,443 votes to out-distance third-place finisher Hicks, who earned 2,560 votes. This was considered a mild upset in itself. But even more exciting, the runoff would pit the veteran politician against the youthful newcomer.

The campaign was well run by both candidates. It appeared from the early beginning that it would be Warsham's stronghold of Alabama City against Means and his door-to-door

Steve Means was elected Gadsden's mayor on September 4, 1974. Mayor Means was sworn into office on October 7, 1974.

campaign throughout Gadsden. The final vote count was 8,006 for Means and 6,671 for Warsham. Actually, Means would have to face a Republican opponent in the September general election.

The general election was held on September 4, 1974, with Democratic nominee Means meeting GOP hopeful Joseph Lee Childs. Steve Means scored a landslide victory, out-distancing his opponent by an 8-to-1 margin. The final vote count was 8,595 to 1,129. Mayor Steve Means was sworn into office on October 7, 1974.

Another dramatic change came to downtown Gadsden in the 1970s with the construction and opening of the Gadsden Mall. The first shopping centers had come to the area during the early 1960s with the construction of the Agricola Shopping Center and the Noccalula Shopping Center, but the Gadsden Mall brought a whole new concept of shopping to hundreds of people.

Shopping took on a whole new look on July 31, 1974, the day that the Gadsden Mall celebrated its grand opening. Construction of the multi-million-dollar mall began in March 1973, but site preparation began as early as November 1972 on the huge project located at the intersection of South Fourth Street and Rainbow Drive. This preparation included the rerouting of utility lines, both gas and electric. The original plans for the new mall called for a Sears, Belk Hudson, and Pizitz stores. Colonial Properties, the owner of this new shopping mall, estimated that shoppers would be drawn from as far away as 30 to 50 miles.

The Gadsden Mall opened on July 31, 1974, and a crowd of 25,000 to 30,000 were on hand for the grand event.

Actual construction of the mall began in March 1973, and all the work, including a huge parking area that could accommodate 3,000 cars, was completed by June 1974. The total available store space totaled 44,303 square feet, and most of it was leased long before the mall was completed.

The Gadsden Mall opened its doors on July 31, 1974. Mall manager Steve Held noted that this gala opening was one of the largest grand openings ever held by Colonial Properties; the crowd was estimated at between 25,000 and 30,000 people. Fifty-five stores, shops, and services opened on that first day, which was actually a day or two earlier than had originally been scheduled. Seven other stores opened within the next two weeks.

Many of the first-day shoppers were very excited about the prospects of shopping in the enclosed comfort of the mall. A person could come to the mall and spend an afternoon or a Saturday morning shopping, eat at one of the restaurants, or take in a movie at the mall theaters. Once a person got inside, he or she could shop without having to worry about the weather. Shoppers no longer had to travel to Birmingham or Huntsville to visit a mall now that there was one here at home.

The coming of the large department stores to Gadsden brought another change to the area. On opening day at the mall, there were suddenly many empty buildings on Broad Street in downtown. Two large department stores, Sears and Belk Hudson, had closed their locations and moved to the mall. Hagedorn's and Ike Sak's also opened stores in the mall and eventually closed their downtown stores. This trend of businesses moving out of downtown would not be reversed for many years.

The opening of the Gadsden Mall and its Twin Cinema also signaled the decline of Gadsden' Pitman Theatre. The Pitman was the last remaining theater in Gadsden until the construction of the Gadsden Cinema at the Agricola Shopping Center. The Gadsden Cinema was a plush 863-seat theater that was constructed at a cost of $200,000 by the Georgia Theatre Company. With the opening of this movie house and the coming of the Gadsden Mall Twin Cinema, the Pitman Theatre saw its reign as Gadsden's last downtown theater coming to an end. With the arrival of the new multi-screen theaters combined with the Pitman Theatre's age, it would only be a short time until this theater closed its doors, although the theater's management vowed to keep its doors open as long as it was economically possible.

In the early days of summer 1976, Gadsden was getting ready to celebrate a special birthday. The entire county was preparing for a celebration that lasted for four days, July 1–4, which were set aside for the celebration of the country's bicentennial.

The 200th anniversary of the founding of the nation was celebrated with two colorful events at Murphree Stadium (one patriotic and one religious), a fun birthday party at Noccalula Falls, and a historic pageant at Carnes Recreation Center in Attalla.

The kickoff for the bicentennial weekend came on July 1 at Murphree Stadium. The presentation that night was entitled "Let Freedom Ring" and was the largest production ever staged in Gadsden. The outdoor spectacular, with a cast of hundreds, ran for three nights. The script for this production was written by Barbara Klein, Dean Cress, and Glenda Byars. Ron Townsend directed the production. The presentation had an almost continuous musical score performed by a 70-piece honor orchestra, which consisted of outstanding high school musicians under the direction of DeLeath Rives.

The bicentennial was celebrated with a costume contest at Noccalula Falls on July 4, 1976.

A family-fun event billed as the "Great American Birthday Party" was held at Noccalula Falls Park on July 4th. The party featured a barbecue, a watermelon-eating contest, a turtle race, a costume and beard contest, square dancing, crafts, bluegrass bands, and other fun activities. The party had an intermission at 5:00 p.m. to allow participants to attend the religious rally at Murphree Stadium. After the rally, the audience was invited to attend a spectacular fireworks display set for 8:45 p.m. at Noccalula Falls.

The chairman for the bicentennial weekend was Dr. O.B. Sansbury, and the Reverend W.H. Granger was co-chairman. Churches in the Etowah County area canceled Sunday evening services to allow members to attend the religious rally. The keynote speaker for the rally was Gadsden's own U.S. Senator James B. Allen.

As the spectacular fireworks display came to a close and the festivities drew to an end, many people stopped to give thanks for the 200 years of freedom that had been enjoyed by all Americans.

Less than two months later, a tragic event in the form of another of the decade's major fires occurred. Probably the most unforgettable fire of the 1970s happened at a small gas station on U.S. 278 near the Gadsden–Hokes Bluff city limits. This fire began on August

31, 1976, when a large tanker was refilling an above-ground storage tank. A spark ignited a large fire that quickly spread and burned out of control.

Several units of the Gadsden Fire Department answered the call, including medics from the Central Fire Station. After a fierce battle with the flames and many anxious minutes, the inferno appeared to be extinguished. Just as the firefighters were approaching to investigate the above-ground tanks, a huge explosion occurred. The storage tanks were completely destroyed and three Gadsden firefighters were killed in the blast. Gadsden Fire Chief Ralph Speer and paramedics Michael Patrick and Michael Thornton were killed instantly. In a brief moment, three brave firefighters gave their lives in the line of duty.

The City of Gadsden remembered these three gallant heroes in a way deserving of one who lost his life in the line of duty. The Central Fire Station was renamed the James R. Speer Central Fire Station and markers were placed at the station to commemorate the sacrifices made by Speer, Patrick, and Thornton.

Also of note in the 1970s were the many national chain, or fast food, restaurants that came to Gadsden; these businesses would slowly replace the privately owned and home-operated establishments that had been so popular during the 1950s and 1960s.

One popular place to eat in downtown Gadsden was a Mexican restaurant known as El Burrito, which was located in the 300 block of Broad Street for many years. This restaurant offered tacos, burritos, salads, and several types of combination dinners. Sunday afternoons were always special at El Burrito because anything on the menu could be purchased at half price. This special was also offered on one week night and was very popular.

Local drive-ins such as the Chow Time slowly disappeared with the coming of the major fast food restaurants.

Probably one of the most popular restaurants during the 1970s was the Panorama Restaurant, located on Meighan Boulevard. The Panorama was the place to go for elegant dining during the 1970s, and when Etowah County was voted wet, the Panorama was one of the first local restaurants to open a lounge.

Other local restaurants to fade into history during this decade were the Mexican Chili Parlor and Mr. Good Guy. The Mexican Chili Parlor had long been a downtown landmark and a favorite place for people working downtown to eat lunch.

Drive-in restaurants that were popular in Gadsden as well. These restaurants were famous for the great hamburgers and milkshakes that they offered. Some of the more popular drive-ins were the Pic-a-burger and the Chow Time. The Pic-a-burger was famous for their Paul Bunyan Burger, which was a large hamburger with a secret sauce, fries, and onion rings. The Chow Time offered a Chow Burger in three sizes. These restaurants were also known for their curbside service.

The Biff Burger was another locally owned drive-in that closed when the large chain restaurants arrived. These national chains, such as Burger King, Hardees, and Captain D's, brought a new concept in convenience food but also marked the closing of many family-owned restaurants.

The 1970s were a turbulent time for the city of Gadsden, a time of great change for both the city and county. The residents of Gadsden had chosen a mayor that would lead them through the remaining years of the twentieth century and into the twenty-first. Decisions were made concerning the sale of alcohol in Etowah County that would have far-reaching effects on the local economy. Large chain stores, shopping centers, malls, and fast food restaurants also emerged, helping to create a combination of old and new businesses that would carry Gadsden ahead on the road to becoming an All-America City.

10. THE ALL-AMERICA CITY

Gadsden evolved quite a bit in the final two decades of the twentieth century. Many new and exciting things came to the city, and several others faded into the city's long and colorful history.

The Gadsden area became the set for a made-for-television movie during the summer of 1980. This movie, filmed on location in Gadsden and Jacksonville between August 18 and September 19, premiered in February 1981. The movie, *Mayday, Kent State*, was a joint effort of Interplanetary Productions and Osmond Communications.

Gadsden State Junior College was chosen to be the site of this movie because of its many similarities to Ohio's Kent State University, which was the scene of a major protest during the 1970s and the Nixon era. Hundreds of Kent State students were protesting America's involvement in the Viet Nam War, but when their demonstrations became violent, the Ohio National Guard was sent in to restore order to the college campus. Following several confrontations between guardsmen and students, an incident occurred in which four students were killed. The movie was based on James Michener's *Kent State: What Happened and Why* and *The Kent State Coverup* by Joseph Kelner and James Munves.

Filming began with the opening scenes on location at the dormitories of the campus at Jacksonville State University. Other filming sites included South Twelfth Street, where several vacant buildings were painted and transformed into downtown Kent, Ohio. Gadsden State Junior College, with a few minor changes, became Kent State University. Other filming sites included the Federal Building on Broad Street and some private residences that were transformed into fraternity houses.

The filming of this movie brought added income to the Gadsden area. A production crew of more than 100 people was in town for more than a month preparing for the production as well as during the actual filming. A support cast of close to 1,000 extras were also employed during the filming of many of the scenes.

The total budget of the production was $4.5 million. Of this budget, between $3 million and $3.5 million were spent in the Gadsden and Jacksonville area. This included the paychecks that many local "students" and "guardsmen" received. For one month, the Gadsden State campus was busy building sets, shooting scenes over and over, and even burning the Kent State ROTC building. Many actors and actresses

Gadsden was turned into Kent, Ohio, when the made-for-television movie Mayday, Kent State *was filmed here in 1980.*

came to town in hopes of getting the boost that their careers needed. Some local residents picked up extra money by either dressing in jeans and becoming a college student or putting on a uniform and carrying a rifle as a National Guardsman.

When the filming was over and everything was packed up and gone, people waited anxiously for the first showing of *Mayday, Kent State.* The film was originally shot as a four-hour docu-drama. After the filming was complete, it was decided to edit the film down to three hours to be shown on one night rather than two. Many scenes were edited out and shortened, although the final film was an exciting and high-quality production.

While Hollywood made a stop in Gadsden during 1980, the first days of 1981 witnessed the end of an era for the movie theaters in Gadsden. January 9, 1981 was the beginning of the end for the Pitman Theatre because on this date, the theatre's management began to operate on weekends only. The Pitman remained open, operating on this schedule for quite some time, although it was obvious from the outset that people preferred to go to the cinemas that were getting the first-run movies. The decision was finally made to close the Pitman. The theater shut down and stood vacant for several months.

The Pitman Theatre was briefly opened for a one-week period in 1983 when a film series was shown there between September 27 and October 2. The film series was sponsored by the BIGMEN and Gadsden Theatre, Inc., and the Pitman was completely refurbished for this special week. The final movie in this series was *Singin' in the Rain,* starring Gene Kelly and Debbie Reynolds. The Pitman stood vacant for many years after this and fell into a state of disrepair. The property was finally purchased by the City of Gadsden for $26,000 in 1986.

In 1983, a new bridge was constructed across the Coosa River. A spur from Interstate 59 through Gadsden that intersected with George Wallace Drive required the construction of a new bridge near Rainbow Drive and the Gadsden Mall. The contract was awarded on February 8, 1983, to an Opelika firm to begin work on this third bridge's foundation within 45 days. The construction of the foundation took a total of 210 days. State Highway Director Ray Bass announced that Briggs Construction Company was awarded the $721,000 project.

The foundation for the new bridge and a series of piers were built with state money from the Coosa River Fund. To build piers for the bridge, steel sheets were driven into the riverbed and the underlying rock drilled out and blasted. Concrete was poured into the foundation area and the water was later pumped out from the box formed by the steel sheet and supports.

A single, 48-foot-wide structure was the initial bridge in the construction of this primary east-west route through the city, but future plans called for a two-structure, six-lane bridge extending Interstate 759 across the Coosa. The State Highway Department had embraced and rejected plans for this new bridge across the river for several years. A joint effort by the Etowah County legislative delegation, city officials, and the business community succeeded in persuading the state to proceed with the project.

The form of city government in Gadsden also changed in the year 1985. Originally, Gadsden had a mayor-alderman form of government. The early mayor was known as

In 1983, a new bridge was built across the Coosa River, connecting East Gadsden and Interstate 59.

an intendant, and aldermen were elected to represent each part of the city. Later, this structure was changed to a mayor-commission form of government, in which a mayor and two associate commissioners were elected by the city's registered voters. In 1985, plans were underway to change the city's form of government once again.

On April 30, 1985, a group of concerned citizens gathered at the Etowah County Courthouse to discuss a proposed bill that would give the city commission the authority to change Gadsden's form of government. This public meeting was called by the members of the Etowah County legislative delegation who planned to introduce a bill in Montgomery that would allow the city to adopt a five- or seven-member council with each member being elected from a separate district.

This bill was drawn up after a lawsuit seeking to change Gadsden's form of government had been filed in the U.S. District Court in Birmingham. The suit was filed jointly by members of the Etowah County Voter's League, the local chapter of the NAACP, and the Southern Christian Leadership Conference. This suit claimed that at-large commission elections discriminated against the city's black population.

Mayor Steve Means and Public Safety Commissioner Tony Reynolds were in favor of the bill, but Public Works Commissioner George Sizemore favored passing a bill that would give the public a chance to vote between a five-member council or keeping the city commission form of government.

After the passage of the bill, it had to be adopted by the city commission and was later approved by the Justice Department. Following approval of this bill, city elections were set. The city election of 1986 not only brought a new council form of government, but a new mayor as well.

Gadsden Mayor Steve Means lost the race that year to Gadsden businessman David Nolen. Nolen had run for mayor in 1982, losing to Means without a runoff. In the 1986 election, however, Nolen turned the table on Means and defeated the incumbent without a runoff. Nolen served the city for the next four years during the transition from the mayor-commission form of government to the mayor-council form of government. Nolen did not seek reelection in 1990, and Means, once again, was elected to the city's highest office. The first people elected from the seven council districts were as follows: District 1, William Cunningham; District 2, Doug Weems; District 3, Robert Avery; District 4, Bob Echols; District 5, Holley Arbery; District 6, Jim Armstrong; and District 7, Lewis Fuller.

Candidates Avery, Echols, and Nolen won without a runoff. The other races were extremely close, and history was made when the District 6 race was decided by only four votes. Arbery was the first woman elected to public office in Gadsden, and Avery and Cunningham were the first blacks elected in Gadsden. Three members of the first city council continued to serve their districts throughout the 1990s. Echols, Avery, and Weems kept their seats on the council as the city of Gadsden moved into the twenty-first century.

During the late 1980s, a concerned group of Etowah County citizens saw a need to honor the fallen heroes of the many wars in which the United States had been involved. This group sought to erect a monument that would serve as a lasting tribute to those who had paid the highest price for America's freedom.

This group was headed by retired Brigadier General Clarence F. Rhea, as chairman, and retired Colonel Andrew A. Chaffin, as executive vice chairman. Other members of the committee included retired Lieutenant Colonel Lloyd Wagnon, Rebecca Vinyard, and retired Sergeant Major Joe Barnes.

This memorial, known simply as the War Memorial, was constructed in 1988. It was designed by W. Clifford Arbery and built on Lookout Mountain near Noccalula Falls. This memorial pays tribute to the different branches of service in which the men and women of this nation have served.

On the interior of this memorial, beneath its rotunda, is a listing of the hundreds of fallen heroes and the war in which each one served. The list includes 73 natives of Etowah County who died during World War I, 282 during World War II, 29 during the Korean Conflict, and another 74 during the Viet Nam War. There was also one who fell in Lebanon, bringing the total to 459 local heroes who died during military action. Today, this lasting memorial stands on the mountain near the Kiwanias Pavilion and is a constant reminder of the ultimate sacrifice that so many have paid in the service of their country.

A joyful event in 1990 served as the culmination of several years of planning and hard work by a group of local citizens and business leaders. On January 7 of that year, at 1:00 p.m., Gadsden's Center for Cultural Arts opened on the corner of Fifth and Broad Streets. For six long years, a group of concerned citizens had worked to help this dream become a reality.

The Cultural Arts Foundation was formed in May 1984 solely for the purpose of building, maintaining, and operating the center. The Cultural Arts Foundation started out with just eight people. They ordered a survey and found that Gadsden wanted a centrally

The War Memorial was built to honor Etowah County citizens killed in times of war.

Under construction in this 1987 photograph, the Center for Cultural Arts was built in the former Belk Hudson building.

located hub for entertainment. During the next several years, the foundation set about formulating plans to raise funds and to make real the dream of a Center for Cultural Arts in Gadsden.

In April 1987, an ideal site for the center was chosen. The former Belk Hudson's building, which had been vacant since 1974, was centrally located and offered ample room for the many things that the center hoped to offer. The foundation made an offer of $300,000 for the building, although its owner at that time, Coosa Federal Savings and Loan Association, was expecting a price of close to $405,000. After further negotiations, Cultural Arts Foundation chairman Jamie Sledge recommended buying the property.

In October 1987, architect Preston Phillips of New York unveiled his model of the Gadsden Center for Cultural Arts at a meeting of the Cultural Arts Foundation. This plan involved a radical redesign of the 44,000-square-foot interior of the former Belk Hudson Department Store. Tommy Phillips of Preston Phillips Architecture in Bridgehampton, New York, planned the center over a six-week period using information compiled from a four-year survey of the 13 local arts groups and civic and service clubs.

The design of the center included large multi-purpose public rooms for dinners, shows, and social affairs. Plenty of storage room was included for equipment needed in theatrical productions. A soup and sandwich cafeteria was planned for the northeast corner of the downstairs floor. Located upstairs were the administrative offices, a museum to house permanent displays, a gallery for temporary displays, and the Original Native American Museum and exhibit space. This area was also to contain a detailed model train display. The structure was in very good condition, and the estimated time projected to transform the building into the Center for Cultural Arts was eight months.

An evening of black tie, glitter, and music filled the center the night before it was to officially open. A dinner dance, the Black and Gold Gala, was attended by more than 600 people, who came to dance to the music of Peter Duchin and his orchestra. The following day, the center was open for the public to see.

This facility was the culmination of six years of hard work for many people in the Gadsden area. On opening day, the center had already been booked for 95 social events. This was only a small indication of the many great things to come for the Center for Cultural Arts.

During the summer of 1990, football lovers in the Gadsden area once again got excited about professional football. On July 28, the season opener for the Alabama Raiders marked Gadsden's entry into the American Professional Football League. This league was like many other minor league systems throughout the United States, which gave former college players and National Football League (NFL) hopefuls a chance to showcase their talents before NFL scouts.

The Gadsden team, known as the Alabama Raiders, was the fulfillment of a lifetime dream of local businessman John Ritchey. During the three seasons of the Raiders' existence, Ritchey fielded a very competitive team, which compiled a record of 39 wins and only 2 losses. The Raiders had an experienced coach in Jim Hilyer and a talented group of local players as well as an exceptional quarterback in Joey Hester.

On opening night, a crowd of more than 4,500 fans was on hand to see the Raiders take on the Phenix City Colonels at Murphree Stadium. The Raiders handed the visitors a sound beating, winning 31-0. This was the beginning of a perfect regular season in which the Raiders won ten games. The Raiders eventually lost the National Championship to the Palos Hills–Orland Park Force at Stagg High School in Chicago. This was a 21-14 defeat for the Raiders, which had seen ten of its players not make the trip because of a tryout camp with the Birmingham Fire of the World League of American Football. The Alabama Raiders took league championships the next two seasons and continued to bring exciting professional football to the Gadsden area.

The weather made the news in a major way during the early days of March 1993. Although springlike weather was being enjoyed during the first week of March, a startling weather forecast faced the Gadsden area on March 12. The forecast called for rapidly cooling temperatures with a chance of snow and freezing rain. Snow with an accumulation of up to 3 inches was predicted north of Birmingham, with up to four times that amount in higher elevations.

On Friday evening, March 12, a light rain began falling in the Gadsden area about sundown. With dropping temperatures, the rain turned to sleet and eventually to snow. Most people went to bed that night wondering what the following day would have in store for a city that rarely experienced a significant accumulation of snow and ice.

What everyone awoke to the following morning was something of a surprise. A deep blanket of snow covered everything. What was predicted to be a 3- to 4-inch snowfall in the Gadsden area turned out to be at least a 12- to 14-inch accumulation, with Boaz on Sand Mountain actually getting around 18 inches of snow. Snowdrifts of up to 3 feet brought travel in the area to a standstill. The temperature continued to drop with the low hovering between 0 and 10 degrees on Sunday, March 14.

The snow, ice, and falling temperatures were only the beginning of the problems in North Alabama. Thousands of people were without power and telephone service due to falling trees and tree limbs. National Guard units, along with local rescue squads, transported elderly and handicapped people to shelters throughout the area. For the next several days, the people of Gadsden continued to dig out of this crippling snowstorm. For some, it would take up to two weeks to have power restored to their residences. In all, there were at least nine reported fatalities in North Alabama during the blizzard of 1993. This total would have no doubt been much higher if not for the efforts of so many—an excellent example of the way people gave a helping hand to those in need.

The Gadsden area was an exciting place to be during 1996. It was during this time that the city celebrated its 150th birthday, or sesquicentennial. These celebrations began on July 4, 1996 and concluded on October 12.

The morning of July 4, 1996, was a special day in the city. This was the kickoff for the celebration, and the festivities began at 10:40 a.m. with a reenactment of the USM *Coosa* landing, which took place on July 4, 1845. The *Coosa*, captained by James Lafferty, landed here, and less than one year later, the city of Gadsden was founded.

The *Alabama Princess* played the part of the USM *Coosa*, and many Gadsden residents, dressed in clothing of the era, took part in the reenactment. Following the landing, a historic marker was unveiled by Mayor Steve Means and dedicated nearby. This marker was co-sponsored by the City of Gadsden and the Etowah Historical Society.

The grand finale of the July 4th celebration and Gadsden's sesquicentennial kickoff took place at 9:00 p.m. A grand fireworks display brought the day's events to a close, and

Gadsden was hit with a blinding snowstorm in March of 1993 with 12 to 14 inches of snow falling in the city.

Gadsden's sesquicentennial parade was held on October 12, 1996.

the people returned to their homes, having learned a little about the founding of Gadsden and the beginnings of this great city.

The festivities in honor of Gadsden's 150th birthday concluded with a day-long celebration on October 12, 1996. Activities began early on Saturday morning with a huge parade down Broad Street. The streets were lined with thousands of excited spectators, many of whom waved American flags and cheered as more than 100 floats, marching bands, and automobiles passed by. The grand marshals of the parade were Tom and Doris Gadsden of Holly Hill, Florida—descendants of James Gadsden, for whom the city is named. The theme of the parade was "Proud of Our Past, Confident of Our Future."

In the parade were many memorable floats depicting events from Gadsden's past. The Goodyear clocktower, Emma Sansom, the Memorial Bridge, and a riverboat were represented on the floats. Many members of the Etowah Historical Society also rode atop the floats in the parade, which was coordinated by Dr. Glenda Selman.

The impressive finale to the day's festivities came in the form of a huge fireworks extravaganza. The world-class fireworks show, which was staged from the Memorial Bridge, took place high above the Coosa River with thousands of spectators watching from below. A total of 4,500 blasts were featured. Two stationary light shows built on scaffolds on the bridge began and ended the show. On one stand was the sesquicentennial logo and on the other was a huge birthday cake that said "150th" on it. The last of the fireworks put a bright exclamation point on the celebration of Gadsden's 150th birthday that had begun more than three months earlier.

Another big event following the celebration was the unveiling of Gadsden's Spirit of American Citizenship Monument. This structure, which towers 67 feet above the river, was built due to the hard work of Peter Gregerson Sr. and the other Sesquicentennial Committee members.

This frosted glass, steel, and granite monument was unveiled on the evening of August 2, 1997. The idea for the monument was born during Gadsden's sesquicentennial celebration. An elaborate dedication ceremony was held; it included patriotic music from the play *In This Valley* and concluded with the lighting of the monument.

A major downtown revitalization effort began on Broad Street on May 15, 1998. Alabama Governor Fob James was on hand, as was Gadsden Mayor Steve Means and several other city officials, for a ground-breaking ceremony held at the start of this facelift. The plans called for a major resurfacing project, wider sidewalks, old-fashioned street lamps, benches, and trees to adorn the landscape. The original plans called for the project to be completed within six months, giving Broad Street a whole new look.

Work began on May 26 in the 500 block of Broad Street with the removal of the top layers of the street's paving, which also exposed the streetcar tracks that had not been used since the streetcars made their final run in the early 1930s. With the removal of this paving, the first problem of the project was exposed. Cracks in the street's foundation caused the project plans to be modified to include the removal of the original brick paving. The streetcar rails were also removed at this time, as were the existing sidewalks and the streetlights. When the repairs were made to the foundation of the roadway, a layer of

The Spirit of American Citizenship Monument was unveiled on August 2, 1997. This monument grew out of the Gadsden Sesquicentennial Celebration.

asphalt was put down, and the new sidewalks and brick pavers were laid to create the wider sidewalks.

As the preliminary work was done in each block, the project progressed east toward First Street. When this work was finished, the final paving was then put down to complete the job from Sixth Street to First Street. The new electric street lamps were also installed in each block as work was completed. The focus then shifted to the 600 block of Broad Street.

With the work slowly drawing to a close in September 1999, the downtown project, which had been estimated to take only six months, had moved into its second year. The final street lamps were being installed, new benches were being placed up and down Broad Street, and the painting was completed in each of the intersections. The new street signs were also in place, which helped to bring a touch of the days gone by to the Broad Street area.

For close to a year and a half, work had progressed on the Broad Street project, and many problems had been encountered, from cracked street foundations and old wells to the remains of Tunnel Block and underground springs. These problems had caused numerous delays in the completion of this project and the cost escalated to $2.4 million. But when it was finally completed, the downtown area had taken on a new look. Many old storefronts had also been restored to their original beauty, adding to the appeal of the revitalization project results. The Broad Street Project was completed under the supervision of Cathy Back and Downtown Gadsden, Incorporated.

The Gadsden area was soon shocked by an announcement made on February 4, 1999—the Goodyear Tire and Rubber Company's Gadsden plant would cease production of tires by the end of the year. Just as surprising, though, was an announcement in October that talks between Goodyear and Local 12 of the United Steelworkers of America

Broad Street was dug up during a major revitalization project that began on May 15, 1998.

Pictured here is the new look of downtown Gadsden following the completion of an extensive facelift.

were underway to continue tire production. That statement was proven true on October 15, 1999, when the company and union formally announced that the company would continue production and call back between 400 and 500 laid-off workers.

In February, plant manager Richard O'Dell made the announcement that meant more than 1,300 workers would be facing layoffs. The plant would continue to mix rubber for other Goodyear plants, and local employment would be reduced to between 200 and 250 employees. An earlier layoff had been announced in November 1998 that had affected 390 workers. With these earlier layoffs and the ones planned to occur by the end of 1999, the total number of affected workers would exceed 1,800 of the plant's 2,000 employees.

The future plans for the Gadsden facility only called for the rubber-mixing operation, storage space for tires, and storage space for tire manufacturing equipment in case the company decided to resume tire production at a later point. Officials said that the decision to end tire production in Gadsden was based upon Goodyear's effort to rationalize manufacturing around its most efficient plant operations. The 70-year-old Gadsden plant was deemed one of the company's least efficient plants. The Gadsden plant did, however, have a state-of-the-art carbon black system that had recently been installed, and its rubber-mixing capabilities were much greater than at most of the other Goodyear plants.

During six special sessions between October 11 and 14, Local 12 members voted by a 3-to-1 margin to approve an agreement with the company to continue tire production. On October 15, officials announced that light truck tire production would continue and passenger tire production would be added.

Gadsden's Gulf States Steel plant would close in the year 2000, bringing unemployment to hundreds of workers.

Just when the situation at Goodyear was beginning to stabilize, the Gadsden economy suffered a massive jolt when Gulf States Steel filed for Chapter 11 bankruptcy in July 1999. The giant steel producer had been one of Gadsden's largest employers since the plant had located in Etowah County in the early 1900s. The steel plant had opened in 1904 with a blast furnace and four 50-ton open-hearth furnaces.

During the next 95 years, the steel-producing giant had undergone closings, reorganizations, changes of ownership, and bankruptcies. The plant had grown, and many improvements were added during the 1950s, when the company experienced record sales and production. During the latter part of the twentieth century, the company experienced declining sales due to the influx of foreign steel; this signaled the beginning of the end for Gadsden's steel mill.

In July 1999, Gulf States Steel filed for bankruptcy. Several cost-cutting measures were put into place in an attempt to keep the plant open, but in June 2000, the management of Gulf States Steel announced a $6.9-million loss for the month, thus casting an even darker shadow on the company's existence in Gadsden.

An attempt was made to secure government loans to keep the plant in operation. These loans hinged on a new union contract between labor and management. This contract called for several concessions by the rank and file, which included wages and benefits. On July 29, 2000, members of the Steelworkers Local 2176 voted down the union contract by an overwhelming majority of 749 to 223. The steel plant was completely closed down shortly thereafter.

During the 1990s, a local artist and retired firefighter made an important contribution to preserving local history as well as to a local charity. Leo Reynolds lived and worked most of his life in Gadsden, where he and his wife, Ruth, had raised their twin girls, Elaine and Jane, and son Craig. Leo was the fire marshal for the City of Gadsden for a number of years; he was also a self-taught artist. In the 1970s, Reynolds began entering art shows in Alabama and several other states as well. He won many awards with his artwork and had several prints on the market. On many occasions, he donated a painting to be "auctioned" for a worthy cause.

In 1995, Leo was approached by the Etowah County Chapter of Easter Seals about providing them with a painting that could be used to create a Christmas ornament, which would be marketed to raise money for Easter Seals. The ornaments would depict objects of historical importance in Etowah County. For the first ornament, Leo did a painting of the statue of Emma Sansom. The project was so successful that it was continued. Other ornaments included Noccalula Falls, the Goodyear Clock Tower, Gulf States Steel, and the Hokes Bluff Ferry. Leo passed away in 1999, and a painting he had already completed was used for the 2000 ornament—the Broad Street, or Memorial, Bridge. Leo's son, Craig, also a very talented artist also, took up the project, and the 2001 ornament is the *City of Gadsden*, a riverboat that once plied the waters of the Coosa River.

In 1999, the Etowah County Law Enforcement Memorial was formed. This non-profit corporation was established by a group of law enforcement officers, their families, and supporters for the purpose of erecting a memorial to honor law enforcement officers who died in the line of duty within Etowah County and to promote law enforcement interests within the county. The City of Gadsden donated a site for this memorial at Noccalula Falls. The monument sits upon a rocky cliff above the waters of Black Creek on the campground side of Noccalula Falls and is constructed of white southern granite. The highest point of the five-point star reaches 7 feet into the air. The lights mounted in the base reflect off the white granite star and glow over the falls at night. The monument includes brick pavers encircling its base. The Etowah County Law Enforcement Memorial

Noccalula Falls is captured in one of Leo Reynolds's beautiful Easter Seals ornaments.

The Etowah County Law Enforcement Memorial is dedicated to officers who have given their lives in the line of duty.

officers include Donna McCurley (president), Jimmie Entrekin (vice president), Wayne Hammonds (secretary), and Paulette Chandler (treasurer).

The names of 16 officers who have fallen in the line of duty are also engraved on the points of this monument. These include Gadsden police officers D.J. Kinney, Charles Gordon Cox, Richard Perkins, and Jimmy Ray McKiven; Attalla police officers Pink Jenkins, Henry Ingram, Grover Pearce, and C.L. Starling; Alabama City police officer William A. Patterson; Etowah County sheriff's deputies Ernest W. Birt, J.O. Johnson, Charles Cook, and Chris McCurley; Alabama state troopers Arvil O. Hudson and Ormand F. Watkins; and Immigration and Naturalization Service officer John S. Starratt. A candlelight vigil is held on the second Saturday in May of each year at the memorial. When the memorial was dedicated, 12 names appeared on the monument; another four names were added the following year.

Over the years, Gadsden has grown and many honors have been brought to the city. One of the greatest of these was Gadsden's recognition as an All-America City. This honor was awarded on June 8, 1991, by the National Civic League at a banquet in San Antonio, Texas. Gadsden had been a finalist for this award the previous year and was one of only two cities to be a repeat finalist in 1991.

Today, the city of Gadsden is growing and evolving with the times. The city that started as the beautiful dream of three men has grown into an important city in Northeast Alabama and one of "America's Most Livable Cities."

Selected Bibliography

Books and Publications

Barnes, Joe. *Gadsden, Alabama: A Short History*. Gadsden, AL: Santos Printing, 1992.

Crownover, Danny. *Black Creek Southern Lookout Mountain*. Gadsden, AL: M & F Printing, 1983.

Etowah County Centennial Committee. *The History of Etowah County*. Birmingham, AL: Roberts & Son, 1968.

Dwight Manufacturing Company. *Alabama City: Its Location and the Advantages It Offers the Working Man*. Alabama City, AL: Dwight Manufacturing Company, 1900.

Martin, Will I. *If Memory Serves*. Cleveland, TN: Banner Print, 1952.

Nevile, Bert. *Steamboats on the Coosa River in the Rome, Georgia, Gadsden, Greensboro, Alabama Trades: 1845–1920*. Selma, AL: Selma Printing Service, 1966.

Woman's Club of Gadsden. *Gadsden: A Little Book about Gadsden, Alabama*. Gadsden, AL: Department of Archives and History of the Woman's Club of Gadsden, 1938.

Newspapers

The *Gadsden Daily News*
The *Gadsden Evening Journal*
The *Gadsden Times*
The *Messenger*

INDEX